Slingshot

Slingshot

*The Fast Track to Financial Freedom
in Auto Repair*

DAVID DICKSON

Innovation Press

San Francisco

For my generous mentors, friends, and clients

CONTENTS

Preface

In NASCAR racing, a "slingshot" is using draft, momentum, and experience to move rapidly past your competitors and into the lead. Whether it's done by a crafty veteran or a ballsy rookie, the driver hangs back until just the right moment and then shoots to the front just in time to take the checkered flag.

It looks easy, but performing a slingshot takes skill, preparation, and good instruction. The reason this book is called *Slingshot* is because a slingshot is not just a racing move. It's a business move too. *Slingshot* describes how I rapidly grew my one small auto repair shop into a chain of twenty-one stores, sold the chain, and retired. And, more important, it describes how you can do the same.

Most auto repair shop owners don't experience a slingshot event because they lack knowledge, encouragement, and vision, but it's not their fault. The shop owners I've worked with are honest, reliable, hardworking people. Most don't even dream that a slingshot event is possible for them. Nobody ever has given them permission to leap to the front. Others have worked hard and looked for success, but they never have found it.

I'm here to tell you that any shop owner can have a slingshot experience—and I mean *any*. Shop owners who've had ten years of no growth produce 20-30 percent gains *year after year* using the simple, straightforward secrets presented in this book. Shop owners who were teetering on the edge of bankruptcy (myself included) have become free of debt within one year. Again, all they did was apply the simple, straightforward suggestions in this book.

Today, I can hop in the plane and fly myself to Key West for the weekend, compete against other world-class athletes in a triathlon, or just get up in the morning and enjoy the fact that I have no obligation to go anywhere or do anything that I don't want to. You deserve the same, and I'm going to tell you how to achieve this kind of lifestyle.

First, here's my story.

I bought my first repair shop in 1998. I had no clue what I was doing. I was in trouble from the day I walked in. I had a service writer who was late for work every day. I had a mechanic who had $70,000 worth of tools but couldn't change a spark plug without breaking it off or stripping the threads. Making the situation even more wonderful, the mechanic had a charming little quirk—he passed out when he saw his own blood. Yes, every time he scraped his knuckles we were gettin' out the smelling salts and pickin' him up off the floor. Then there was the muffler guy who never wore safety gear. Every time he put on a muffler we got to watch him do a little dance when a piece of slag would get into his pants or shoes. Oh, I almost forgot about the other mechanic, who would run out the back door and down the street every time a police car pulled in for a speedometer check. Did I mention the fact that I was pretty sure one of them was stealing from me? Yep, it was a pretty sad situation all around.

I started out losing money and I just kept on losing it. Lots of money. It seemed like I was always just one piece of equipment or a clever advertising slogan away from turning the corner, but it never happened. Pretty soon I was taking credit card advances just to make my payroll. I was scared to death.

Now let's fast-forward three-and-a-half years. I was working no more than five or ten hours a week (that's right, a WEEK!). I had twenty-one auto repair shops. I was wealthy.

I didn't have employee headaches. I traveled whenever I wanted to, which usually was about once a month. I could go to Key West, Phoenix, San Francisco, Dallas, the Bahamas ... wherever I wanted, whenever I wanted. My life was very low stress and lots of fun!

Today, my life is even better. I'm retired at the ripe old age of 46. I've successfully sold my chain of shops and I have total and complete freedom in my life. I can do whatever I want, whenever I want. I can indulge my passions (which happen to be helping others duplicate my success, competing as a top-level amateur triathlete, and flying). Life is good, but I never forget that all this is possible because I learned how to effectively operate one independent auto repair shop.

So how did I finally turn that corner and end up with all those shops, each of which ran like a well-oiled machine? It started with a couple of great mentors—and they told me some incredible secrets. They taught me how to pay attention to my business. They taught me how to market. I stopped spending money on worthless advertising and spent it on powerful marketing. They taught me how to pick the right jobs, to send those worthless, time-consuming, profit-robbing jobs down the street to one of my many competitors and make lots of money on the ones that I kept. They taught me how to fire bad employees and hire great employees. They taught me how and what to say to customers to earn more money.

Before I decided to embrace and follow my mentors' advice, I made $18,236 my first year in business. By the end of my second year, after discovering and implementing the advice from my mentors, my business skyrocketed. I had gross sales of $997,786. Wow! I didn't believe it myself until my accountant told me I had to write a check for an extra $90,000 in taxes—and I had the money to do it! I was on my way. I am today a very wealthy man entirely because of the good advice I was given.

Here are some of the incredible things my mentors taught me—the very same slingshot secrets you'll discover in this book:

- How to capture up to 70 percent gross profit

- The simple steps that guarantee you'll hire only great employees and chase away the bad ones

- A Sales Success System that will make 95 percent of the customers who walk through your door eagerly accept all the repairs you recommend

- How to get what you need from bankers, parts suppliers, and tool guys—without letting them run your business

- Duplicate yourself so you can own as many additional shops as you want (or just make one shop hyper profitable) almost effortlessly, spending less time than you now spend with only the one shop

- How to know when it's time to get out, how to sell your shop, and to whom you should sell it

- The attitudes and actions that ultimately destroy most shop owners

- How to free yourself from day-to-day operations—no more wrench turning

- The four marketing techniques that will slingshot your business to profitability and why they work

- How to answer the phone and make money on every single call, no matter what the customer says

There's much, much more, and it's all right here in this book. I've cracked the code. I have the password. I know the secret handshake and I'm willing to share it with you! WHY? To make good on a promise I made to my mentors.

When I was struggling to get started in this business, I had three incredibly talented and interesting people as mentors—a tough-as-nails ex-highway patrol officer who had been shot six times, a spiritually connected but intensely realistic business leader, and a street fighter in the business world.

I would have never made it without their help. And at some point, each one of them made me promise that if fantastic success came to me I would pass along the knowledge and experience that had created my success. They actually said that the only way to continue on to greater success was to share this knowledge—and to help others become incredibly successful just like me.

As you can probably tell, I'm not a professional writer— actually, I hate writing. I have the attention span of a gnat and I'm about as creative as an accountant (no offense if there are any accountants reading this). But I am a man of my word. I said I would pass on the secrets and that's what I'm doing.

Despite some initial reluctance to write, I decided it just had to get done. This book is my chance to give back to an industry that has been incredibly good to me, even though I certainly didn't feel the love the day I started.

I started the "giveback" phase of my career by mentoring hundreds of shop owners from all over the country. Big shops, little shops, multiple shops, and single shops - they've all experienced their own slingshot events. Shop owners who were filled with fear and self-doubt have found the secret to building not just their businesses, but their courage and self-confidence.

This book and the resources provided in it will give any shop owners access to all the knowledge, encouragement, and vision they need to create their own slingshot experiences. Hundreds of shop owners already have done it, using exactly the same secrets and simple techniques described on these pages.

The keys are in your hands. Your hot rod is sitting in the driveway. So turn the page, make a couple of simple adjustments, and see what your baby can do!

CHAPTER 1

10 Reasons Auto
Repair Shops Fail

I used to drive race cars. Years ago, I had a shop at Sears Point (now Infineon Raceway), just outside San Francisco. One day I was at the track, watching a practice. As the pro was coming down the back side of the track at top speed, he lost control of his car. He spun and then crashed violently into a concrete barrier. The car was destroyed and I honestly thought he had been killed. The rescue workers were there within seconds and quickly unbelted him and got him out of the car. He was a little wobbly, but he seemed OK otherwise. He stood still for a minute, and then he did something amazing. He started walking back up the track, looking at his skid marks, trying to figure out what he had done wrong to cause the crash. Wow! He actually was using a near-death experience as a learning tool. He was so committed to getting better at what he did that even a disaster was an opportunity to learn.

While growing my auto repair business from one shop to twenty-one shops, and while coaching hundreds of other auto repair shop owners, I've watched and experienced plenty of "near death" business experiences. I've seen way too many shop owners fail. Let's take a walk back up the track and see why these disasters happen.

Ten Reasons Why Auto Repair Shops Fail

1. Poor Marketing
2. Poor Sales
3. Hiring the Wrong People
4. Inefficient Shop Flow and Production
5. No Effective Support System or Relationships
6. Fatal Attitudes: Beliefs That Destroy Profitability
7. Fatal Actions: Actions and Inaction That Kill Any Chance for Profit
8. Time: Not Respecting and Managing the Only Nonrenewable Resource
9. No Exit Strategy
10. Lack of Clear Vision or Goals; No Strategic Plan

1. Poor Marketing

In the "good old days," all you had to do was rent a building (or just set up under a nice big tree) and hang out a sign that said "We fix cars good!" If you did this, and you could do a decent job of fixing the cars, you'd have all the business you needed. You would make enough money to buy a nice house, buy a couple of nice cars, send your kids to a good college, and maybe take a fun vacation every year.

Those days are OVER! And they will never be back. Twenty percent of the auto repair shops that were in business in July 2006 have failed and are out of business today. Twenty percent! Average annual sales have dropped almost 5 percent and continue to fall steadily. The average repair shop will do only about $250,000 in *gross* sales. By the time you take out rent, parts cost, and employee payroll, if the owner is lucky, he or she will have made $35,000. If you want to succeed, you must have a marketing plan.

Your marketing plan must be simple, easy to implement, and based on proven and effective strategies. You can't waste time or energy trying to reinvent the wheel or discover the next big thing. The good news is that if you can focus on four simple tools, virtually all your marketing needs will be met. That's what I'll explain in my chapter on marketing, but don't skip to that yet!

2. Poor Sales

This one is tragic and widespread. Your marketing is working and people are coming through the door, but there is no money in the bank at the end of the week. Your service writer seems busy, you make a lot of friends and help a lot of people, but you're going broke. Sound familiar? Your sales process is failing, usually because someone is confusing being nice and friendly (which is a good thing) with actually selling something (which is a very deliberate, step-by-step process).

I'm a pilot. When I talk to air traffic control, I'm really not looking for a friendly and warm greeting. I'm looking for information that will keep me alive! When someone comes into your shop with a broken car, he or she is looking for someone trustworthy to fix it. If the customer gets a warm and friendly greeting, it's a pleasant surprise. Some of the best service writers are like air traffic controllers. They are personable and they know how to build rapport, but it is crystal clear when you hear them talk that they have one mission—they are out there to solve each customer's problem by selling him or her a *profitable* solution!

Too many times shop owners say, "I just can't find a good service writer." I say, "Then make one." The average customer says no five times. The average salesperson asks for the sale twice. Who do you think is winning this battle? The process of selling service is simple. The problem in most shops isn't a lack of natural sales ability (which is a highly overrated characteristic); it's the lack of a systematic approach to the selling process. You have to have a carefully planned way to get past all the "nos" and get to the "yes." In the chapter on selling you'll find a simple six-step system that will get you a "yes" every time.

3. Hiring the Wrong People

Bad people, or good people in the wrong positions, quickly will put an auto repair shop out of business. The service writer who can't sell or the technician who can't fix cars is dangerous and damaging. The real tragedy is that shop owners put up with these people. Why do they do this? Fear. Shop owners keep the wrong people because they don't have confidence in their ability to find better people. They are terrified of losing the person they have, even if that person is doing a horrible job, because they don't have a system and the tools to find a replacement.

That's over. In the chapter on people you'll get both a system to use and the tools to make it work. You'll discover the four best ways to get a steady stream of job applicants. You'll learn how to screen and interview these candidates. Then you'll learn how to use pay plans and other powerful tools to keep the good ones with you forever. And, because I know this is the hardest of all, I'll give you an easy process that allows you to confront and, if necessary, painlessly fire an employee who is not a good fit for you. With these resources your fear will turn into excitement. Instead of wondering where a bad employee's replacement is going to come from, you'll have five to ten people lined up and waiting to come work for you. Instead of having constant turnover, you'll have people who stay with you for five, ten, or twenty years. This process changes everything.

4. Inefficient Shop Flow and Production

This one is like high blood pressure. It's a silent killer and there are usually no symptoms until it's too late. Of the 20 percent of shop owners who went out of business in the past two years, a huge number of them failed because of inefficient shop flow and poor production management.

Customers standing around asking the technicians questions (or making arrangements for the tech to fix the car at his house on Sunday for half the price), parts sneaking out the back door (and into employees' cars), expensive real estate (the bays and lifts) sitting empty and idle. These are problems of inefficient shop flow and production management.

Most shop owners have never even stopped to consider shop flow and production management. The cars come in, the technicians work on them, and then the cars go out when they're done. That's the way it always has been. Well, it's time for a change.

You have to look carefully, step-by-step, at what happens when a car comes into the shop. How does it get brought in? What happens to the customer? What happens to the car? You'll see in the chapter on shop flow and production how to easily and logically do this. It's all outlined in a simple nine-step plan.

5. No Effective Support System or Relationships

This reason for shop failure is particularly sad. It reminds me of a story I've heard several preachers tell over the years.

A devout God-fearing man is out fishing in a boat. There is a terrible storm and the boat sinks. Since he is a devout man, he figures that if he prays God will save him. So he prays for a miracle. Shortly after he finishes praying, a piece of wood floats by. The man thinks about grabbing the wood, but he remembers praying for a miracle, so he lets it go by and he prays some more. A few minutes later, a boat spots him and pulls up to get him out of the water. He tells the people on the boat that he's not going to accept their help, because he prayed for a miracle and he's gonna wait for it. He prays some more. Then a Coast Guard helicopter arrives. A diver jumps into the water and the crew lowers a basket, but the man refuses to get in. He repeats that he's prayed to God for a miracle and he's gonna trust God and wait. The man is exhausted. He no longer can stay afloat and finally he drowns. However, he's a devout God-fearing man, so he goes to heaven. When he gets there he's confused, so he says to God, "I was a devout man, I lived a good and honorable life, and yet when I needed you the most you didn't deliver a miracle." God says, "I sent you piece of wood, a boat, and a helicopter! What more could I have done?"

The preacher's point, of course, is that there are miracles being delivered to us every day. We just don't recognize or utilize them.

This lack of ability to recognize and utilize the support systems and resources that are easily available and in fact all over the place is what causes many shop owners to fail. There are experts in every area who are ready and willing to help, and yet so few actually are used. All the support necessary to grow and sustain your business is out there. You just have to take advantage of it.

You never should have to wonder how much money you have in the bank. You never should wonder how much profit you made last month. You never should have to feel your heartbeat quicken when you get a letter telling you that you're being sued. You never should have that nagging doubt about whether you're getting the best deals on your parts or tools. You should have the resources to give you confidence and certainty in each of these five key areas.

In the chapter on resources I show you how to stop praying for a miracle and instead get the most out of the five most valuable resources and relationships you have as an auto repair shop owner.

6. Fatal Attitudes:
Beliefs That Destroy Profitability

What we believe has a huge impact on how we act and the results we achieve. We either create or we sabotage our success by the attitudes and beliefs we hold.

You've probably heard the urban legend about the guy who accidentally gets locked in a refrigerated boxcar. He dies and the people who discover his body find a note detailing how he slowly froze to death. The kicker? The refrigeration unit on the boxcar wasn't working. The only reason he froze to death was because he believed it was cold.

In the chapter on fatal attitudes you'll cover the six attitudes and beliefs that make a lot of unsuspecting shop owners "freeze to death." The good news is that these attitudes easily can be fixed. Once you have this awareness, the correction is easy.

7. Fatal Actions:
Actions and Inaction That Kill Any Chance for Profit

Ultimately, everything revolves around action. If you do the right things, you'll get fantastic results. If you do the wrong things, you'll get disastrous results. Unfortunately, nobody ever seems to be specific about what the "right" things are.

In the chapter on fatal actions you'll discover the six things to do (and not do) to create the greatest possible profit in the shortest amount of time—without shortchanging yourself or your business.

8. Time: Respecting and Managing the Only Nonrenewable Resource

Is there a sense of urgency in your shop? I hope so, because a lack of urgency is a lack of respect for time. And lack of respect for time is deadly. Failing shop owners think they have all the time in the world to turn things around and solve their problems. They don't. Time is precious. Time is limited. Time is nonrenewable.

Most people think money is their most precious resource. They are wrong. Money is like a huge river constantly flowing by. You can dip into the river with an eyedropper, a five-gallon bucket, or a tanker truck. It doesn't matter, because the river still will be there flowing strong.

Time is like driving down the road toward a destination in a car with no gas gauge. You know the engine is getting gas now because it's running, but you never know when you're going to run out.

You never know when you are going to run out of time, both personally and professionally. It's a waste to spend too much time thinking about this. Control what you can. Feather the throttle. Maintain a steady speed. Decrease the load on the engine. Take the shortest route. In other words, do everything you can to get the most out of the time you have.

In the chapter on time you'll get seven key tools that will "increase your mileage" and allow you to radically increase what you are able to do in a given period of time. If you use these tools as described, you will find yourself accomplishing more than you ever dreamed possible.

9. No Exit Strategy

So many shop owners are bummed out, burned out, and buried. I know you know someone like this. He hates to get up in the morning, absolutely dreads the thought of going into the shop, and then when he gets there is buried and discouraged by the work in front of him.

Have you ever talked to him about what he plans to do for retirement? "Retire? I'll never be able to retire. I don't know how to sell this thing and get my money out."

These are all signs of someone without a good clear exit strategy. Lack of an exit strategy is a major reason for auto repair shop failure. Too many times, shop owners just slowly go out of business when they could have realized huge financial windfalls from their assets (their shops) that they have taken decades to build and nurture. In the chapter on exit strategies you'll get an easy solution. You'll know if you should sell, when you should sell, and to whom you should sell. You can finish the game wealthy and successful or poor and defeated; it's up to you.

10. Lack of Clear Vision/Goals

All these actions, attitudes, tools, key concepts, and techniques are useless unless they are tied to a clear vision and to a set of goals that support the vision. Once you have these two things in place, the path to success (the "right" action) is clear.

Look, it's simple. If your plan is to show up every day and fix whatever cars happen to come into the shop, then you eventually will fail. Unfortunately, this is how most shop owners operate. That's why most auto repair shops don't last past one generation.

The good news is that since you have this book in your hand, you have the tools to escape this trap and move forward. When the topic of vision or goals comes up, most people's eyes glaze over. They think they need to worry about getting the best price on parts, not on describing a vision. But don't fool yourself. Having a clear vision supported by goals with a plan to execute is the only way to build a business that will grow and survive.

Clarifying your vision and goals is not impossible. In fact, it's easy. In the chapter on vision and goals you'll get four simple questions that will clarify your vision and then five easy steps to set the goals that will help you make your vision a reality. And you'll avoid one of the most common reasons auto repair shops fail.

So we've clearly defined the problem. You've seen for yourself the ten reasons why auto repair shops fail. Now that you understand the problem you face, let's get to the solutions.

CHAPTER 2

Marketing

I bet you hate spending money on marketing. When I started my slingshot, I did. I always wondered whether my marketing was actually working, and I was uncomfortably aware that it probably wasn't. You probably feel the same way. Back then, I didn't have a plan. I just sort of let the ad reps find me, and when somebody suggested something that sounded good, I gave it a try. The good news is that once you develop a system that's simple and effective, and actually tracks your marketing success, all your marketing worries will go away. You'll know which ads to run, and you'll know immediately if they are working. You'll know how much money to spend to make a certain amount, and you'll know exactly where to spend it.

Four Simple Steps to Effective Marketing

There are four simple steps to effective marketing.

1. Identify Your Market

2. Develop a Compelling Message

3. Track Your Results with a Simple System

4. Deliver Your Message through Several Different Media

1. Identify Your Market

With hundreds of clients all over the country, I see financial statements and sales reports from every area. I've seen some very consistent results across the country, which is why I can give you some very important insights into identifying your markets.

Geography

Eighty percent of your clients will live or work within a two-mile radius of your shop. This has been confirmed over and over again. People will not travel much farther than a couple of miles for auto repair. If you really understand this concept, it will shape and focus your marketing decisions. You should not be advertising all over your city or town. You need to maximize your marketing in this vital target zone.

Demographics

More than 50 percent of the people making buying decisions are women. Most of your clients will be over thirty, working-class, low- to mid-income people. Their cars are generally more than five years old and they'll visit your shop three or four times a year. You need to get your name and your shop in front of as many local working-class people with five-year-old cars who live or work within two miles of your shop as possible. And you need to do it as often as possible, using as many methods as is practical. Think about how this knowledge changes where you spend money. You probably won't use *Fortune* magazine. You probably won't even use the regional paper. However, a monthly newsletter would be perfect. We'll talk more about this in a minute.

If you want more help deciding how to target your marketing, visit me at www.DavidDickson.com/guide.

2. Develop a Compelling Message

If people don't even know you exist, how can they possibly give you their money? Marketing is the act of getting noticed. And more than that, it's about developing a compelling message. The average person is exposed to approximately 3,000 ads per day. To stand out from this crowd you've got to be compelling. A friend of mine used to say, "To stand out you must be really pretty or really ugly; everything in the middle is ignored." Keep this in mind when developing your message. When you sit down to work on your marketing plan or a marketing piece, there's one important question you must ask yourself, "Will this get me noticed?" If the answer is "yes," you are on the right track. If the answer is "no," then you need to find another approach.

Whole books have been written on the subject of developing a compelling message, but let me give you the shortcut here: *It's something you do better than anyone else.* Are you more conveniently located? Are you faster than the competition? Do you offer loaner cars? Are you more experienced? Do you have better equipment? Do you give away something special with every repair? I had one client who lived near Chicago and he would go plow the driveways of his best customers after a snowstorm. Those people were never going anywhere else. He owned them. He did something special and unique - definitely something to talk about. What makes you special may have seemed ordinary to you, or it may be something you've been doing for a long time and never really talked about.

I'd suggest that before you start giving stuff away, differentiate yourself with a story. People love stories. If there is something unique about you, your family, or your history in the area, you have a fantastic tool for getting people to connect with and remember you.

For example, I'm a pilot. I'm rated in instrument flying. I can fly aerobatics, seaplanes, and twin-engine planes. I've had my license since I was seventeen years old. I love to fly. When I tell people this, they almost always want to know more or they want to tell me about someone in their family who flies. That's great, because it means they are connecting themselves with my story; we've actually bonded because of this shared experience. If my ad has a bright airplane graphic, the people who see it say, "Oh yeah, that's the guy who flies planes!" They're immediately primed to see me in a good light and they feel like they know me—which means they feel that they can trust me.

If you don't have something special to talk about, create it. You could have a hot dog vendor set up his cart in your parking and sell nickel hot dogs; that'll give your customers something to talk about. You can do a free brake promotion (go to www.DavidDickson.com/guide to find out more about this incredibly effective promotion). If you do, believe me, people will talk about it. Give a lifetime warranty (you can see how and why you should do it at www.DavidDickson.com/guide) on every repair. Do something that makes you special. Do something that makes you stand out.

3. Track Your Results with a Simple System

You can't make good decisions if you don't know whether your money is working for you. The best way to track your marketing efforts is to have your customers do it for you. For instance, if you send out a flyer with a coupon for a free oil change, all you have to do is save the coupons as they come in. Once the promotion is over, you simply total up the number of coupons and the amount of money you made. I know a shop owner who has a big wall in his office; he takes all the redeemed coupons and staples them up there, along with a piece of calculator tape that records the cost and return of each campaign. He can walk into the office, look at the wall, and immediately see which campaigns worked and which ones didn't.

You should pay attention to dollars made, not necessarily the number of people who responded. In most cases, the dollars are much more important than the overall response. Your tracking system doesn't have to be high tech; it just has to work. If the final number is positive or close to positive, it was a successful campaign and you should do it again and again.

4. Deliver Your Message through Several Different Media

So you've got some great stories, something special and compelling to talk about, and you know how you're going to track your campaign. Now how do you get it out there? I've tried hundreds of different marketing strategies and techniques over the years, and I've seen other shop owners try thousands more. Here are the top four. Let's call them foundation marketing strategies. If you execute them completely and correctly, you will have a solid foundation for any other marketing you choose to do; you'll never need to do anything else.

The Four Foundation Marketing Strategies

1. Monthly Newsletter to Customers
2. Customer Care Club

3. Location

4. Networking Groups—Knocking on Doors

They're listed in reverse order. In other words, we'll talk about the best one last.

1. Monthly Newsletter to Customers

If you could go into the living rooms of your best prospects (your existing customers) once a month, sit down with them, and say anything you wanted to say, do you think you would do more business with them? Of course you would. Well that's exactly what you are doing when you send a monthly newsletter. You get to build trust, entertain, and make offers. And customers respond like crazy. It's not uncommon for shops to be booking appointments two and three weeks in advance just days after their newsletters hit mailboxes. As a matter of fact, I have several clients who have divided their newsletter lists into two parts; they mail one part on the first of the month and the other on the fifteenth, just to keep from being overwhelmed with business. This is a high-quality problem, and it's a problem you want.

The key to using a newsletter effectively is consistency. You have GOT to send it out month after month, like clockwork. Too many times, shop owners will send a newsletter out once or twice without tracking the results and then decide that it didn't work. They are sadly mistaken. It takes a couple of months after you start a newsletter to get your clients accustomed to it. Once they are, you'll actually start getting phone calls if it shows up a little late for some reason.

Another important thing about the newsletter is that it can't be all about auto repair. Auto repair is boring to the average person. Joe Average doesn't care—*until his car breaks.* This is why the newsletter is so effective. Even if that customer just looks at it once a month and throws it in the trash without opening it, it's done its job. Once a month, you move from your customers' subconscious minds to their conscious minds. When they find themselves in need of auto repair, they will think of you first. You are training them.

The first thing people ask about the newsletter is, "How do I do it?" Well, you can do it yourself.

All you have to do is scour the Internet for a bunch of good stories and pictures that aren't copyrighted. Next you need to buy and get really good at using a desktop publishing program. Then you need a good reliable printer to print everything and get the completed newsletters to the post office. Of course, a lot of printers don't deal with the post office, so you might have to handle that yourself. The line usually isn't too long. Ha!

Are you getting the picture? You don't want to have to mess with this. The good news is that you don't have to. There is a great resource for producing newsletters. I've worked with her for years and she is bulletproof reliable. Plus, she has an online system that takes less than fifteen minutes of your time each month. Think about it, a fifteen-minute investment and you've got one of the four key marketing tools that will slingshot you from flat broke to wealth and success. If you want to add this powerful marketing weapon to your arsenal, just go to www.DavidDickson.com/guide and you'll see how easy it is.

2. Customer Care Club

The next tool on your list should be a Customer Care Club. People love to be in clubs. People love to get special discounts. People love to feel like they're set apart from the crowd. That's the whole idea behind a Customer Care Club.

All you do is make up a card consisting of a series of coupons. Usually, these include four free oil changes and then six or eight other offers—10 or 15 percent off any repair, $20 off brakes, free A/C inspection, or whatever else you'd like.

I can hear you doing the math in your head, trying to figure out if you can handle that kind of loss. But here's the deal—you're not giving these coupons away. You're selling them at the front counter. Your service writer offers it to every customer for about a hundred bucks. Shops all over the country are doing this every day. All the service writer has to do is explain that for $89.95 you get four free oil changes PLUS all the other stuff, and he or she pushes the fact that the free oil changes alone pay for the card.

I've sold as many as twenty of these a week. Clients of mine have sold forty in a week. That's an extra $1,800-$4,400 per week *without any immediate parts or labor costs attached!* You can make hundreds of thousands of dollars with this tool, and it's the gift that keeps on giving. The customers will come back at least four times for the oil changes, so you get to inspect their cars four more times for other repair opportunities. If you are not using this tool, you should be. You've just seen how to do it. If you think it's a great idea but you're afraid you'll procrastinate and not get it done, just go to www.DavidDickson.com/guide. You can do everything online and have this powerful moneymaking tool in your hands in days.

3. Location

Location is your next top marketing tool. I don't care where your shop is. Whether you're on Main Street with a giant sign or in a low-traffic industrial facility (or in your driveway!), your location still is important.

If you are in a high-traffic area, your location should be your biggest draw. Make it happen. Have fresh paint, a fresh parking surface, and great landscaping, and make sure everything is clean, clean, clean. A friend of mine used to say,

"You wouldn't wear a tuxedo with brown shoes. You shouldn't miss any details when it comes to making your shop stand out." Many people paint the building but forget to refresh the parking lot or spruce up the landscaping. Instead of the fresh paint making the shop look better, it actually makes it look incomplete and unfinished. Always make sure the whole package looks good. Park across the street and just stare at the shop for a while. If anything stands out or doesn't look clean, modern, fresh, and more on the upscale side, go fix it.

Now that your shop looks great, draw attention to it. I've used flags, air dancers (those fabric slips with a fan inside) and sandwich board signs. The best attention-attracting device ever was a bubble machine. It's cheap, unusual, and eye catching. Just one suggestion—if you use a bubble machine and place it out by the street, chain it to something. I can't tell you how many bubble machines we lost to "grab and run" thieves.

Your town won't let you use flags? Your zoning is too posh for air dancers? Flags of countries almost always are allowed. Put out a large U.S. flag and then two or three flags representing the largest ethnic groups in your area. In one of my shops we flew the Mexican and Canadian flags along with the American flag. The visibility it created and the response it generated was fantastic.

Anything you can do that draws attention, in a good way, increases the value of your biggest marketing investment.

4. Networking Groups—Knocking on Doors

Most shop owners instinctively resist when I tell them about this marketing strategy. Too bad, because you are your own best marketing tool. People do business with people they like and trust, and they like and trust people who talk to them face-to-face. Plus, once you practice a little and get good at it, it's a lot of fun and you meet people who can be incredibly helpful as you grow your business.

Many clients say, "But Dave, I'm not a good speaker. I don't like to talk to people. I don't 'mix' well." Trust me, I understand.

If you met me, you'd swear I was an extrovert who loved being around people and enjoyed the limelight. I'm not. I'm an introvert who relishes peace, quiet, and long solo walks on the beach or the company of one or two close friends.

But that doesn't matter when it comes to marketing a business. You can train yourself to be good at mixing. You can train yourself to speak reasonably well in front of people. You can train yourself to communicate really well with people, mostly by listening.

The key to marketing yourself is to get out there. You don't have to change who you are. You don't have to give up a piece of yourself. You simply acquire skills that are important to your business success. The good news is that it's really easy to do.

So where exactly do you go? Any local service club is a great place to start. I started going to Sertoma and Rotary club meetings and the customers started coming in immediately. They're still coming in to this day. Go to Business Networking International meetings. If speaking even to small groups intimidates you, join a Toastmasters group. Or start visiting local businesses. Before you know it, you'll have more customers than you can handle.

Want a technique that doesn't take up any of your evenings? Want one that gives you a little vacation from the workday? I'll give you that and more—and it involves pastries! Visiting local businesses *during the workday* is by far the most effective one-on-one marketing strategy I've ever used. Here's how it works. Go out and get two dozen doughnuts or other individual pastries. Then go get a bunch of the plastic clam shells that delis use to put food in. Put two doughnuts in each one. Once the morning rush at the shop is over, hop in your car with six or seven of these little customer-seeking pastry bombs. Walk into a local business with one of your doughnut packages and a business card (you also can bring a flyer). When someone greets you, simply say, "Hi, my name is (insert your name). I own (name of your shop) right up the street. We're a full-service shop and we do everything from tune-ups and brakes to engine replacements. I just wanted to stop by, drop off some doughnuts, and introduce myself. Is there anything I can do for you today?" That's it. Those five sentences formed the foundation for my auto repair empire. If you're willing to do this, you'll get more valuable customers from this one strategy than any other one you've ever used - so many, in fact, that after ninety days you'll probably no longer need to do it.

If you visit ten businesses, at six of them you'll probably recite your short speech, drop off the doughnuts, say thank you, and then leave. However, at the other four someone in the office will say, "Hey, my car is making this funny noise …" or "You know, I'm due for an oil change and brake job. When could you get me in?" When this happens, all you do is pull out your keys and say, "Why don't I just leave my car here and take yours back to the shop. I'll look it over and call you; I won't charge you a dime for checking it out." The guys at the shop will get used to you coming back with cars other than your own. As a matter of fact, if one of your guys isn't busy, don't be surprised if he comes up and asks you to go out "hunting."

Why does this strategy work so well? Two simple reasons: First, you're approaching potential customers in a very direct, honest, and helpful way, and you're giving them something of value (doughnuts!). It's just natural for them to want to give you something in return (their business). Second, they get to meet you on their own turf. This is very nonthreatening. They get to see you as a normal businessperson, probably a lot like them, people who are trying to build their businesses. What you are doing makes sense to them. They empathize with you and want to help by giving you their business.

Never go to more than five or six businesses each day. Usually, you won't have to visit more, because by the third or fourth stop you'll be driving someone else's car back to the shop. But even if you don't, five or six stops are enough. You don't want to be away from the shop for more than a half-hour or so. The best time to do this is between ten in the morning and two in the afternoon; after the morning rush and before customers need to pick up their cars in the afternoon.

So there you have it, the only four marketing strategies you'll ever need. However, if you think you might want more, just go to www.DavidDickson.com/guide. I have direct mail pieces, flyers, inserts, and all kinds of other tools that have made me and my clients lots of money over the years.

CHAPTER 3

Selling

If you cannot sell service effectively, and cannot hire and manage someone who can, you will go broke! It's just that simple. Without sales talent at the front desk, you're dead.

I've personally sold more than a million dollars in service in a single year at the front counter. I've successfully managed service writers who have sold more than a million dollars a year. What I'm about to tell you is not some sales theory made up by some sales trainer who has never actually sold anything. Everything in this chapter is the result of real-world experience, tested and verified by me as well as by shop owners all across the country who are just like you.

Hire Sales Talent or Do It Yourself?

If you're just starting out and you have the ability to talk to people, you really should do the selling yourself—at least for a while. You'll save a ton of money and aggravation, and you'll gain personal experience in the most vital position in your shop.

If you hire sales talent, you've got to learn to make quick decisions based on performance. If your salesperson is performing at an acceptable level, then everything is fine. If he's not, then you either need to give him some training or replace him. Immediately. Which one you do should be based on his success and performance before you make your decision. Remember, you're paying a salesperson. If your salesperson is working well with customers and technicians, then he may be worth the investment in training. If he is struggling with these basics, it may be better just to replace him.

Train or Fire Your Service Writer?

Unless you change something, nothing will change. This sounds obvious, but you'd be surprised how many times shop owners will say, "I think she just needs a little more time to get comfortable." This is a huge mistake. After the first thirty days that chair is as comfortable as it's ever going to get. If your salesperson is not "comfortable" and is not selling like a maniac within those thirty days (actually, two weeks is more than enough time) then trust me, it's never gonna happen. You need to train or fire.

Selling service can be a difficult and intimidating process. Most shop owners never have taken the time to look at the sales process systematically and to break it down into bite-size chunks, because it's so overwhelming. But if you don't break it down, it's like trying to fix a car or perform surgery with your eyes closed. However, when you follow a system, selling or managing sales is easy.

The Six-Step Sales Success System

There are six points to the Sales Success System:

1. Greeting and First Impression
2. Information Gathering

3. What-Why-When-How Much

4. Overcoming Objections and Closing the Sale

5. Up-Selling

6. Customer for Life Follow-Up

1. Greeting and First Impression

How you greet people sets the tone and is the most important part of the sales process. People buy from professionals they like and trust. The whole point of the greeting is to build rapport. You want the customer to relax, feel comfortable, and like and trust you as a salesperson or—even better—as an auto repair expert and consultant.

The proper greeting starts with a smile. Make the person feel important; pretend that he or she is a dinner guest in your home. People naturally relax and smile back when you smile at them. Then find common ground simply by asking questions. People love to talk about themselves; all you have to do is ask. The best questions deal with one or more of five areas and are open ended. Here are the five: job, vacation, pets, hobbies, and sports. Open-ended questions cannot be answered by a yes or a no. "What kind of work do you do?" or "Hey, where did you go on vacation this year?" are perfect examples. Get them talking about themselves.

The other thing you want to do is to form a connection to their lives. When they talk about their jobs or recent vacations, look for points of commonality. For example, if someone is talking about a trip he or she just took, maybe you visited the same spot two years ago; maybe your cousin lives there. You need to make your prospective customer feel that the two of you are connected, on the same team, bonded. And just like that, you've built rapport with this person.

Everyone walking into your shop should be greeted within fifteen seconds. Even if you are in the middle of something, you should stop what you're doing, look up, make eye contact, smile, welcome the customer, and tell him or her you'll be there in a minute.

You always should introduce yourself by name. The goal here is to build trust. Giving your name before getting someone else's name is an important part of the trust-building process. "Hi, my name is _____. Welcome to _____. How can I help you today?"

Make sure to maintain eye contact when talking to the customer. Nothing is more impersonal than when a service writer talks to a customer while staring at a computer screen. This is a surefire profit killer. Eye contact is one of the sincerest forms of flattery. It tells the person you are talking to that he or she is important to you. It generates trust and creates a feeling of respect in the person you are speaking with. And, critically, eye contact gives you authority and control in the sales process.

It's also important to remember to be polite and professional in your interactions with customers.

This means no profanity (even if the customer is using it). No "tech talk." Don't use industry jargon or acronyms to sound smart or confuse the customer. All this does is alienate the person and make him or her feel distrustful. Another big no-no is flirting. Nothing will destroy trust with a customer faster than being propositioned, especially when all he or she wanted to do was get his or her car fixed. Just don't do it. Finally, don't talk politics. It's not professional and you've got a big chance of being on the wrong side of whatever issue you bring up.

The last piece of a great first impression that leads to a successful sale is being neat and clean. The idea here is to be nonthreatening to the customer. You don't want this person to see anything that causes a feeling of distrust or is visually unappealing.

If you want to have the highest level of visual trust with potential customers, you'll have no facial hair, no visible tattoos, no visible piercings, and no extreme hairstyles. Before you guys with beards and tattoos send me hate mail, remember that this has been proven by study after study. If you want to build *maximum* trust, shave it off and cover 'em up. If you're having success without doing this, then don't worry about it. Just keep doing what works. A clean uniform, a name tag, and a positive attitude are the final key ingredients in a great visual first impression.

Phone Greeting

The customer call is probably the most frequently mishandled part of the greeting and first impression process. There are five steps to handling the phone effectively:

- Use a standard greeting every time.

- Get the caller to bring the car in.

- Always answer within three rings.

- Never leave any customer on hold for more than thirty seconds.

- Smile.

Here is a standard greeting that is particularly effective: "Thank you for calling (shop name), home of the (insert special). My name is (insert name). How can I help you today?"

Here's an example with real names and specials inserted: "Thank you for calling Dave's A/C and Repair. We're currently offering free A/C diagnosis, with less-than-five-minute wait times. My name is Dave. How can I help you today?"

The really great thing about this greeting is that it allows you to talk about a special before the customer even asks a question. Always rotate the special. This keeps it fresh and keeps the service writer from getting bored. Also, the special should match the time of year. Talk a lot about your A/C special in the spring and summer. Talk a lot about brakes, tires, and maintenance in the winter. This is a very effective way to start the relationship. Talking about the special adds approximately two to four seconds to the whole greeting. It's time well spent.

Getting a car in the bay is the only goal of a phone call. Too many times, service writers get into diagnosis, price quotes, and all kinds of other unprofitable nonsense on the phone. The only worthwhile thing you can accomplish on the phone is to get people to bring in their cars. To do this, you have to give them hope and you have to make them feel like you are concerned about them and their issues. Here are my magic words:

"Many times, customers think they have a big problem. Once we look at it, we discover that it was something minor and inexpensive. We never charge for the initial inspection. I can bump another customer a few minutes and get you to see our top tech this afternoon. Can I write your name in the book?"

When I do Service Writer Training classes (if you want to know when the next one is, go to www.DavidDickson.com/guide), I often tell a story about a guy who called me and insisted that he needed a compressor and wanted a price. I asked him a couple of questions, explained that we do free A/C checks, and got him to bring in the car without me giving him a price quote. We checked it out and discovered that he needed a $19 pressure switch, not a $650 compressor. He was relieved, and his case demonstrates exactly why we don't try to fix cars or quote prices over the phone.

There is one exception to my rule about never quoting prices over the phone. You've got to be able to quote commodities (e.g., oil changes, brakes, tune-ups). The best way to do this is to start at the lowest end of the price range, use the word "free" a lot, and never mention how high it could go. "We do tune-ups starting at $29.95, depending on exactly what your car needs. We'll perform a free inspection and we never do any work without asking you first."

Three More Phone Handling Tips

Even if you have to pull one of your techs off a job to put him at the front desk, make sure the phone is answered within three rings. Any more than that and you sound too busy to help the customer. Forget about using an answering machine. If customers are shopping for auto repair and they get an answering machine, they will not leave a message. They'll just go to the next shop on the Google list.

Never leave a customer on hold for more than thirty seconds. If you can't deal with someone in less than thirty seconds, take a number and call back when you have the time to talk.

Finally, smile. Study after study has proven that people can "hear" a smile. Make sure that you, or whoever you have answering the phone, is smiling when you say hello and when you give your standard shop greeting. This is a simple but very effective way to boost profits.

2. Information Gathering

You want to ask questions that uncover the customer's needs and clarify what the problem is.

"What seems to be the problem?" is a great question to start with. Once the customer answers, ask two more questions: "When did you first notice it?" and "Exactly what happened?" The answers to these three questions will give you a pretty good idea of what kind of repair you are looking at.

The next question to ask is, "How long have you owned the car?" This question tells you how committed the customer is to the car and how willing he or she is to fix it. How can you tell? Because the average person keeps a car for about 28 months. The closer that person is to the 28-month mark, the more likely he or she is to get rid of it instead of doing a major repair. (This doesn't mean you won't recommend a major repair; it just means you'll need to be careful about how you do it.)

The last question is a result of painful experience. "Will you be the person approving the repair?" When it comes time to sell, you've got to be talking to the decision maker. How many times have you or your service writer done a great job of presenting a repair to someone, only to have him or her look at you and say, "Great, thanks! I'll go tell my (boyfriend, mother, husband, wife, etc.) what you just told me and I'll get back to you." You **MUST** have the phone number of the person who can make the final decision. You do not want somebody else translating for you. You can guarantee that he or she will mess up the delivery, and the odds are high that you won't get the job.

Throughout the call or conversation, you should practice active listening. This simply means that at several points during the process you summarize what the customer has told you and make sure that you heard him or her correctly. All you have to say is, "OK, let me make sure I understand. You said …" and then repeat back what was told to you. One of two things will happen. The customer either will nod and say, "Yes, exactly!" or he or she will correct you and give you more valuable information. Either way, it helps the process.

It is vital to accurately document the customer's complaint in writing. Let me give you three sample writeups:

- A/C check, need price
- A/C check, car not cooling down well

- Cust. request free A/C check. She says car has not been cold for about two months. Had top-off at another shop, car was cold again, but it only lasted two days.

With the first two, the tech has nowhere to start. With the third, the tech knows exactly where to start and what to look for.

Another important part of the information-gathering process is respecting your and the customer's time. There is more to this step than just asking the customer when he or she needs the car. Of course you have to ask when the car is needed, but you also have to ask why the car is needed. If the customer wants the car back by two in the afternoon to go to a Little League game, you should offer the shop's loaner car and keep his or her car as long as you need. If the customer needs the car back by two in the afternoon to go on vacation, you need to shift things around if necessary and get the job done.

The conversation should end with the most powerful magic words of all: "We offer same-day service. If you drop it off in the morning, in most cases, *unless we have a parts problem*, your car will be ready by five." The problem may be getting the old part off, it may be getting the new part from the parts house, or it may be getting the new part put on. No matter what, it's a parts problem.

If you do this correctly you'll eliminate most of the irritating phone calls from the customer throughout the day. Eliminating these calls makes you much more efficient and you can take on even more work.

3. What-Why-When-How Much

These are questions that must be answered during every repair process. They need to be answered even if the customer doesn't ask them. Especially the "why" question. I'll explain that in a minute, but let's start with the "what" question.

What

"What's wrong with my car?" Everybody wants to know the answer to this question. That's why people bring their cars into your shop. The best answer is the simplest one: "My technician looked at your car and discovered that your _____ is broken/needs replacing." Or this: "My technician looked at your car and he needs to replace _____ before he can complete his diagnosis. This may fix the problem, or more work may be needed." Both of these statements are simple and easy to understand. Using either one of these statements to answer the "what" question will keep you out of trouble every time.

Why

Next comes "why." This is a tricky one. It's tricky because many times the customer won't ask this question directly. Whether the customer asks, however, this question MUST be answered for every repair. If you don't answer this question, doubt will eventually creep into the customer's mind. At some point, often days after the repair was finished and paid for, the customer will question the need for the repair—especially if it was an expensive repair. All you have to do to avoid this problem is use these magic words: "Your car broke because _____" or "I don't know why this problem occurred; it looks like the part just failed. Sometimes that just happens." Don't make guesses when you're not sure what happened. Tell the customer only what you are sure of. And never make something up! The simple, honest, straightforward explanation is always the best one.

When

"When will it be ready?" is the next question most customers ask. The simple answer here is to use the magic words I suggested earlier: "We offer same-day service. If you drop your car off in the morning, in most cases, *unless we have a parts problem*, your car will be ready by five." This eliminates the need for customers to call you five times during the day (although some still will) and ask if the car is ready yet.

How Much

Finally, the biggie. "How much will it cost?" Your ability to answer this question effectively determines whether you make money or lose money and ultimately determines whether you stay in business. Here are the magic words for the cost question: "The total cost of the repair, including parts, labor, and sales tax, is $XXX.XX. Do you have any coupons or are you a member of the Customer Care Club?"

There should be very little pause between the statement of price and the follow-up question about coupons and the Customer Care Club. You will gain useful information from the question, plus it distracts the customer from focusing on the big, bad price. This is vital to the closing process.

Your words must be delivered with confidence and authority. Notice that you are not asking the customer if he or she wants to have the repair done. You are making a statement that assumes you will be doing the repair. If the customer disagrees, he will have to speak up and stop you. Practice is the key to delivering the cost statement effectively. At first, the words may seem awkward, but the more you use them (and the more sales you make), the more comfortable and natural they will become.

If you've followed the process properly up to this point,

then one of two things will happen: The customer will tell you to go ahead and do the repair or he or she will make an objection.

4. Objections: Closing the Sale

At first, every objection seems unique and difficult. However, if you listen carefully you'll realize that you hear the same objection repeated over and over again, with different details. When you carefully break these down, you'll see that there are only five basic customer objections.

- Your price is too high.

- I need it sooner.

- I need to talk to _____.

- I have to wait until _____ to do the repair.

- I'll have get back to you.

Once you can categorize objections, it'll be easy to come up with simple strategies for dealing with each one.

Your Price Is Too High.

Oddly enough, this is the best possible objection you can get. A customer who says this is satisfied with every other part of the transaction. She only wants to negotiate.

Never be intimidated by this objection. When you hear it, you should jump up and down and do a victory dance. This is a great objection. It means that the customer has agreed to have the repair done. She's accepted everything you've told her. She trusts you to do the work. Here are three strategies for profitably handling this objection.

Feel-Felt-Found

Feel-Felt-Found: "I know how you feel. I felt the same way until I found out (the value)." This statement works because the first thing you are doing is establishing sympathy (I know how you feel). Next you establish empathy (I felt the same way), and then you add new information that gives the customer a *face-saving* way to change his mind. Face-saving for the customer is very important because you'll never win a direct argument. If the customer says, "Your price is too high!" and you say, "No it's not!" you'll lose every time. The customer will go somewhere else before he admits that he's wrong.

Here's an example. The customer says, "Your price is too high!" You say, "I know exactly how you feel; I felt the same way when I was quoted this price. Then I realized that was the price for a brand-new part with a lifetime warranty, not a remanufactured part with a thirty-day warranty." This strategy allows you to add information without having to tell the customer directly that she is wrong or is being ridiculous.

The Feel-Felt-Found strategy is a very effective one, and most of the time you won't need to lower your price. This should be the first strategy you use when you encounter a price objection.

Ask Questions

The next strategy is to ask questions. These may include the following:

- Compared to what?
- What makes you say that?
- Why would you say that?
- Do you realize that the price includes _____?

- Do you want the best repair or the best price?

The purpose of these questions is to slow the customer down and maintain control of the sales process. As soon as you ask a question that the customer can't answer quickly, you're back in control.

The first three questions invite the customer to justify his statement that your price is too high. They also give you some idea of what you're working against. For instance, if you ask, "Compared to what?" the customer might say, "The shop down the street said they'd do it for $XXX!" Then all you have to say is, "That's good, but does their price include (value)?" If the customer doesn't know, you've won. Again, the key point is that these questions put you back in control and give you vital information about how the sales process is going.

The next question, "Do you realize that the price includes _____?", is just a shorter version of Feel-Felt-Found. In this question, you skip the Feel-Felt parts and jump right to the part where you add value. Again, this gives the customer a *face-saving* way to change his mind—and we know how important that is.

The last question on the list is a little dangerous. To use this question you need to have a lot of confidence and also some rapport with the customer. This is a challenge question. You're telling your customer that she needs to take her focus off the price, and you're telling her in a very direct, almost confrontational manner. This question should be delivered with a smile. Even with that, some customers will be offended. Be prepared for that if you use this question. It's often helpful to add an analogy. For example: "If you needed open-heart surgery, would you want the cheapest doctor or the best doctor? It's the same thing with this repair." Definitely deliver this one with a smile.

Here are a few more points to remember when dealing with a price objection. First, create benefits; don't compete with prices. If someone is challenging you on price, let him win, by giving him something extra instead of lowering your price (free oil change, windshield wipers, tire rotation, etc.). Create a picture in the customer's mind. If his A/C is broken, tell him to imagine driving through Death Valley with a perfectly functioning A/C system. This may sound corny, but it works. Reduce the price difference to the lowest-possible unit. If your price is $60 higher than that of a competitor, point out that it is only the cost of a cup of coffee at Starbucks each day for the next month—about $2 per day. Point out that you offer much better service: free towing, longer warranty, whatever it is. Train yourself, through practice, always to sell value, not price. Sell service and quality, and be specific.

I Need It Sooner.

This is a fairly easy objection to handle. Don't fight this one. Say simply, "What I hear you saying is that if I could have it done by _____ you'd have me do the repair?" If the customer says yes, then it is up to you to figure out how to get it done. Also make sure you know why she needs her car at a certain time. If it's because she has to be somewhere or do something, you might be able to give her a loaner car or a rental. That will eliminate the time pressure entirely. "I need it sooner" is another "good" objection because the customer is ready to do business with you—if you can solve this simple problem for her.

I Need to Talk to _____.

This objection is tricky. If you get this objection it means that you didn't find out who the decision maker was when you did your information gathering. The best way to handle this objection is with pressure. If you can, use this statement:

"I only can honor this price today because _____. Why don't we call _____ and get his approval?" The "because" is always one of two things: parts availability or labor availability. Thus "I only can honor this price today because I've only got one of these parts left" or "I only can honor this price today because I have a tech available to do it right now." If you use pressure, it always must be about parts or labor availability, but you must never, ever lie about parts availability. If you have one part left or the parts house has only one available, that's fine, but don't lie. It will only come back to haunt you.

I Have to Wait Until _____ to Do the Repair.

This objection is very similar to the one above. Here are the magic words for this one: "That's fine, but unfortunately I only can honor this price today because _____." Or use this response: "Great, I'll schedule you in and take a deposit so I can go ahead and order the part."

With the first statement, you are going to use one of the same two reasons you used in the previous objection: parts availability or labor availability. With the second statement, you are simply accepting the objection and agreeing with the customer. When you do this, one of two things will happen. The customer will agree and give you a deposit, or she'll come up with some reason why she can't leave a deposit. If this happens, you'll know that you haven't found the real objection yet.

I'll Get Back to You.

This is the worst possible objection. When you hear this, what you're really hearing is: "I don't like you, I don't trust you, and I'm definitely not getting back to you." When you get this objection, don't get discouraged. Just realize that somewhere along the line the sales process has gone off track.

There are three ways to handle this: 1. "What if I could show you how you would save 10 percent by doing the repair today?" 2. "Remember, we'll beat any estimate by 20-50 percent." 3. "It's unusual for someone not to do the repair at this point. Is it something about the shop? The price? Me?"

The first two responses are desperate, naked appeals to price. Usually you want to avoid selling on price, but with this objection you're probably never going to see the customer again if he leaves. So it is a good time to make your very best offer.

The last statement is designed to get you back into the beginning of the sales process. If by using it you are able to engage your customer in a conversation, you may have a chance. But you'll have to go back to the beginning, to the rapport-building steps. You'll have to listen carefully to discover why you didn't connect.

5. Up-Sell

The next step in the Sales Success System is the up-sell. There are two types of up-sells. The first happens when you sell an additional service as part of the repair for which the customer came in. For instance, someone comes in for a timing belt and you sell a water pump while you have the front cover off. The other type of up-sell is an offer of something unrelated to the main repair but that has value to the customer and results in more profit for you. An example of this would be windshield wiper blades.

First let's talk about up-sell as part of the repair for which a customer came in. Once the customer has said yes to the repair, you may find something else to sell. It's best to use a good-news, bad-news strategy. Tell the customer something good that you've discovered about the car before you tell her what else needs to be fixed. For instance, "We did the complimentary inspection and found a couple of things. It's no big deal, just _____. You can wait until next time you're in if you want to, but I recommend you do _____ right now to prevent a breakdown or more expensive repairs later."

Here are two magic-word statements to use when up-selling more service. "Let's take care of this now while the car is here so you don't have to bring it back again" and "For just a small investment, you get real peace of mind. Unexpected breakdowns are incredibly inconvenient and can be dangerous. Let's just go ahead and take care of this now, OK?"

Both of these statements give the customer compelling reasons to do the repair that you're recommending.

The first one deals with convenience. Bringing a car in for repair is a very disruptive process. The person has to change her routine that day, perhaps taking time off from work. Most people's lives are interrupted when their car is unavailable. If you can solve a potential problem while the car is already in your shop rather than asking the customer to bring it back a second time, she will be happy and you will make more money.

The second statement deals with safety. No one wants to be "incredibly inconvenienced" or put in a dangerous situation. With this statement, you are reminding the customer of the consequences of driving around with a car in need of repair.

The second type of up-sell deals with offering extra value to the customer while making extra money for the shop. To be successful at this type of up-sell, you only have to ask consistently. It's a lot like when you go to McDonald's and they ask you if you want fries with your burger. In this case, you're going to offer things like windshield wiper blades, Rain-X, an air filter or fuel filter, or maybe an oil change - all things that add value for the customer and are quick, easy, and profitable for you to do.

To be successful at this kind of up-sell you'll need to have a plan and to try at least two up-sells with each customer. Don't worry if the customer says no. Remember, this is "would you like some fries with that burger" selling. Just ask consistently and watch what happens.

6. Customer-for-Life Follow-Up

One of the biggest mistakes shop owners and service writers make is with follow-up. You spent a lot of money on advertising and marketing to get the customer to come into the shop. You put a lot of effort into the sales and repair processes. You've got a huge investment here and yet all too often the follow-up process is ignored. Next to the initial building of trust and rapport, this is the most important part of the sales process.

The first step in the follow-up process is to resell the value the customer just received. Make sure you explain exactly what was done. Make sure the customer understands everything you did, including anything extra you did for free. I usually read right off the repair order. It is also important that you carefully explain the warranty. And don't forget to tell your customer about any smells or noises he might discover that result from the repair. How many times have you put on fresh rotors only to have the customer call you back and frantically say, "My new brakes are smoking!" If you had taken the time to explain, "We cleaned the packing grease off your new rotors, but they still might smoke a little for the first few days," the frantic call never would have happened. Slow down; this is not the place to rush. This is the most valuable time you can invest because the customer is happy and you can set up the next sale. Make sure you answer all questions. Sometimes salespeople are afraid of questions because they might kill the sale; here, the sale already is done, so the pressure is off. Invite questions and take the time to answer them all. Take the time to thank your customer for his business. He had a choice, and he chose you.

Schedule the next appointment! This is the most important step in the follow-up process. There is no time like the present to take care of this. A great analogy is the dentist's office. When you go visit the dentist, someone always will grab you on your way out and schedule your next appointment. Usually, you just stand there and agree to whatever date you're given. You aren't even really thinking about it. But it doesn't matter, because they've got you on the schedule, which means now they have permission to call and remind you. It's the same way in the shop.

Everybody is going to need at least an oil change in the next ninety days. Just go ahead and schedule that. Magic words: "Today is May 1. I'm going to go ahead and schedule your next oil change for August 1. You're a Customer Care Club member, so it'll be free. Should I remind you by phone or email?"

Notice the power of this statement. You are telling your customer that she is getting something for free and you're offering to remind her of the appointment so that she doesn't miss it. You are her hero!

What if she's not a member of the Customer Care Club? Simple: You just change the words to "… If you were a member of the Customer Care Club, it would be free." If she isn't a member yet, there is a good chance she'll join now.

Of course, you start each day hoping that some cars will come in and you'll have a busy day. Once you start scheduling the next appointments and making reminder calls, you can start every day with six to eight cars waiting to get in. This makes a huge difference to your profitability—and your stress level.

Also, at this point you need to make sure the customer is scheduled to receive the newsletter, thank-you letter, and any other communications from your shop. Remember, the stronger the relationship you build with your customers through regular contact, the more likely they are to come to you when their cars break—and the more likely they are to refer their friends.

If you follow the six steps in my Sales Success System you will make your sales most of the time. If your service writer is not selling 90 percent of the people who walk into your shop, then he is doing a poor job. He either needs training (for more information on training, go to www.DavidDickson.com/train) or he needs to be replaced (see the next chapter).

CHAPTER 4

People

If you've got good people, you can handle any challenge. Without good people, the smallest bumps become business killers. Why? Simple. When you have good people you're not in it alone. You have access to more information, knowledge, and talent than you possibly can have within yourself.

If you have an unproductive shop, it's probably because some of your people are a bad fit.

Most shop owners have trouble holding these people accountable and, when necessary, firing them. That's OK. In this chapter you'll get the tools you need to do both of these things successfully.

Four Top Strategies for Finding New Employees

1. Employee Referrals

2. Recruiting from the Competition

3. Help Wanted Ads That Work

4. The Low-Tech Secret

1. Employee Referrals

"Great people" in your shop are those who care about your business almost as much as you do. Great people are the most important ingredients in the profitable operation and growth of a business. Great people attract other great people. Getting great people into your business should be your top priority. So, how do you do this?

The first step is really simple. You approach your best employees (not your worst employees) and you say, "I really like having you here and I appreciate your work. Do you know anyone who you think would be a good fit for us?" Great people know great people, good people know good people, and bad people know bad people.

Find out who your best employees' friends are. Make sure they know that you always are looking to add good people to your business. If one of their good friends is even thinking about making a job change, you want that person to talk to you first. This is a great way to get some absolutely fantastic people. An added benefit is that the training time can be reduced dramatically because the employee who made the recommendation will adopt his friend and make sure the transition goes smoothly. All you have to do is ask. This is how you should start every employee search process.

One more point about getting great people. To get great people, you must be a great employer. If you have a bad temper or are impulsive, moody, indecisive, dishonest, or unreliable, then forget about getting great people. It ain't gonna happen. If you do hire a great person, he won't stay long. This doesn't mean you can't be demanding and have high standards. Heck, great people love these environments. They just have no tolerance for BS.

2. Recruiting from Competitors

The next step in the search process is to look at your competitors. Some people get a little uncomfortable talking about taking employees from the local competition. If your competitors are paying their employees well and giving them good work environments, then nothing you can say or do will entice those employees to leave. If on the other hand your competitors are not paying their people well or aren't providing good work environments, their employees eventually will leave and go somewhere else. If those dissatisfied employees are great people, you want them to come to you.

One of the most controversial strategies for getting employees from competitors is to get your oil changed at a competing shop. While waiting for the oil change you get a chance to watch the people in the shop as they work. It's easy to spot the great employees. When you find one, simply hand him or her your business card and say, "Call me. I'd like to offer you an opportunity to change your life." It never fails. When you do this you'll at least get a phone call. If this sort of recruiting makes you uncomfortable, then don't do it. But remember: If that person is unhappy, he's going to go somewhere else; it might as well be to you!

3. Help Wanted Ads That Work

By far the most common (and hardest) way to get great employees is to run ads and conduct interviews. If you are going to run an ad, make sure to run one that works. All you want it to do is generate leads. Here are three ads that consistently have worked well over the years. The first two are for technicians and the third is for a service writer.

Technician:

Tech wanted, own tools, exp. five-day wk, $2,000/wk, call 555-1212, signing bonus

OR

Auto Mech, $2,000/wk, five-day wk, health plan, holidays and paid vacation, no "heavy" work, $2,000 signing bonus, call Dave at 555-1212

Service writer:

Automotive Service Manager

A progressive, state-of-the-art automotive repair facility is seeking an organized, motivated professional with the ability to effectively communicate with technicians and customers and increase service scheduling, technician productivity, and performance. Full-time position with a five-day workweek. Compensation will be based on experience and ability and will include a benefits package. $3,000 signing bonus is available. Please send cover letter and resume to _____ or call555-1212 to schedule an interview.

These ads have been used successfully in newspapers and online. They work quite well in both places. There are a couple of key elements. The first is the high weekly pay amount. For this amount, use the most that any person has made in that position in the past year. Everybody should be paid for performance, so this is a commission figure.

The second key element is the signing bonus. You should have no problem paying a huge signing bonus to the right person. If somebody comes to work for you, does a good job, and makes you a lot of money, he or she will more than earn the signing bonus. The important thing about the signing bonus is to pay it in a way that doesn't hurt you. The best way is to pay 10 percent of the bonus on the day the new employee starts and then the balance of the bonus on his or her ninetieth day of employment. If this person is as good as you expected based on the interview, this will not be a problem. If it turns out that you made a mistake, you've only cost yourself 10 percent rather than the whole bonus.

4. The Low-Tech Secret

The final recruiting strategy is brain-dead simple and unbelievably effective. Hangout a "Help Wanted" sign. In today's high-tech world, this one regularly is overlooked.

It works because your best employees, just like your customers, are going to come from the area around your shop. They probably live and work close by. Even if they don't read the newspaper or go online to check job listings, they can't miss a big "Help Wanted" sign in your shop's window.

The only difference here is that you have to be ready to interview, or at least schedule an interview, at any time. The sign encourages people simply to walk in and apply.

If I'm not very busy, I try to give walk-ins a quick ten-to fifteen-minute interview right on the spot. If I am busy, I schedule a time when they can come back and interview.

Don't forget to use this simple low-tech tool when looking for great employees.

Screening Applicants

So you run the ads and you get a big response. What do you do now? Ads generally will produce a large number of responses, probably from far more people than you actually want or need to talk to. You need to screen. There is a tool for this: a screening questionnaire. These questionnaires are available at www.DavidDickson.com/guide.

With these questionnaires you can weed out the people who will waste your time. You can focus your energy on the people who might be a good fit for you. So what's the next step, once you've narrowed down the field?

Interview Setup

Interview, interview, interview. Pick a day and schedule six to ten interviews, one after the other, in fifteen-minute increments. Do it at your local Starbucks or some other site away from the shop. Interview salespeople, technicians, assistants, all kinds of people. Interview when you need someone and also when you don't. The key is to keep interviewing. You'll learn several important things by doing this.

First, interviewing will give you confidence. If you're not regularly interviewing, your employees can hold you hostage. When you think about one of them leaving or about having to fire one of them, you'll be terrified because you don't know how to replace people. Get yourself a file full of applications from qualified candidates. You'll have no fear.

Second, you don't always get it right when you interview. You make mistakes in hiring, but you also find some real diamonds. These are employees you can turn into partners and grow with. This process of finding diamonds has very little to do with your skill as an interviewer. Rather, it comes from persistence. You'll find diamonds simply because every Thursday you'll be there at Starbucks wading through the mud, searching. If you search for something long enough, even if you're not the best searcher, eventually you'll find it.

Finally, when you interview you'll learn a lot about your market and your competitors. It's amazing what people will tell you about their former employers (your competition) when you interview them. Million-dollar deals and acquisitions sometimes are based on information learned in interviews.

So, what do you look for on the application? Two things: stability and relevant experience. You want somebody who has held a job for a while. This is less important in today's job market than it used to be, but someone who's been holding on to a job for a reasonable length of time probably has the ability to deal with the ups and downs of daily work. This is important because you're looking for people who are going to stick with you for a long time.

The second thing you should be looking for is relevant experience. Ideally, you want someone who already has been successful doing exactly what you're going to be asking them to do.

The Interview

Let's talk about the interview itself. As I said, it's best to hold the first interviews away from the shop. You need a good environment where you can interview a lot of people in a relatively short period of time. That's what makes a place like Starbucks so good. Schedule someone every fifteen minutes. For a first interview, fifteen minutes is plenty of time. It's best to ask the same questions every time. This way you can focus on the person you're interviewing rather than worry about what you're going to say. A list of the questions I use is available at www.DavidDickson.com/guide.

Once you've done the initial interviews, you can either do a second round with your top picks or just hire directly from the first interviews. Be sure to tell everyone you've interviewed that if you're interested in hiring or re-interviewing them, you'll be in contact within twenty-four hours. Make it clear that if they don't hear from you within twenty-four hours, it means that you're not interested. This is important. It's not fair to leave someone hanging with false hope.

You usually can make a decision about technicians right on the spot. If you're interviewing for a service writer, however, and you have any doubts, just tell the candidate to stop by the shop so that you can talk to him or her again. You should have your shop foreman speak with these people as well. Between the two of you, you should be able to get a good read on someone.

Another important point: When I hire someone, I tell him a story. I tell him that the shop is like training camp for the football season. By passing the interview, he isn't guaranteed a position; he's simply won a tryout for the team. Say he's a receiver; the quarterback is gonna throw him some passes. If he catches them, he gets to stay on the team. If he drops them, he's cut. His ability to stay with me will be based solely on his performance.

Once you've made the decision to hire, there are several important steps to follow and issues to deal with. Here are the top four things you must do to keep good employees.

Four Things You Must Do to Keep Good Employees

1. Align your goals with your employees' goals.

2. Establish pay plans for your workers' performances.

3. Beyond pay: Understand what employees really are working for.

4. Train your technicians and service writers.

1. Align Your Goals with Your Employees' Goals.

So now you've got some great people hired. How do you make sure that they are doing what you want them to do? How do you make sure that your goals and their goals are in alignment? Simple. Share your goals with them and ask them about their goals.

This doesn't have to be a particularly formal process. Every morning when your people get to work, just ask them how they're doing. Ask them what work they need to get done today, and *then* tell them what your goal is for the day. Next, discuss any conflicts or challenges. Then ask them if there is anything they need from you to help their day go more smoothly. Usually, they'll just say, "Lots of easy, profitable work!" That should be music to your ears. When you hear this you know your goals are lined up perfectly!

2. Establish Pay Plans for Your Workers' Performance.

Another way to make sure your goals are lined up is through the pay plan. Your rule should be very simple. As the owner, you are paid for performance (or not, if you don't perform). So make sure that everyone who works for you also is paid for performance. The only exceptions might be for clerical or entry-level positions.

Here are two simple pay plans, one for technicians and one for service writers. Technicians: 15–18 percent of the total ticket, parts, and labor before sales tax. The only exceptions are oil changes, tires, and most dealer parts. You'll see why in a moment.

Service writers: 6–8 percent of the total ticket, parts, and labor before sales tax. The same exceptions apply to them as apply to techs; no oil changes, tires, or most dealer parts. These plans have worked well in big stores and small stores alike. If an employee can't make money on this plan, he's probably not a good fit.

Let me explain the exceptions. You shouldn't pay on oil changes because you don't make any money on oil changes. Oil changes are a commodity; they are not a profit center. They are a reason for you to take a look at the car. That's why a complete inspection sheet is so important on every car (more about this in the next chapter). If you don't make money, neither does anyone else. And if you aren't a tire store, you probably just do tires as a courtesy for good customers. You could pay $5/tire for mounting and balancing, but as with oil changes, if you're not making money, no one else is either. Finally, dealer parts. When I opened my first shop, my guys sold me on how we should use dealer parts on all our repairs. I figured out pretty quickly that I wasn't making any money. Still, they insisted that they needed dealer parts. So I said, "No problem, I'll get you dealer parts. But if I don't make money, you won't make money." As soon as I put this policy into effect, all of a sudden aftermarket parts were just fine!

This information on pay plans should make it clear how important it is to pay everyone for performance. This is one ironclad rule for success.

3. Beyond Pay: Understand What Employees Really Are Working For.

Now that we've talked about pay, let's talk about what your employees really are working for. Money is important to them, but most people work for more than money. It's important to understand this and make sure you're giving your people what they're really looking for.

Once they decide the pay is acceptable, the next thing most people look for in a job is a good work environment. This means a place where they're treated with respect and acknowledged for their skills and accomplishments. It takes very little time and effort for you to do this, and it pays huge dividends.

Greet your staff every morning. Make sure you get to the shop fifteen minutes before they do. When they arrive the doors should be open, the lights should be on, and you should be ready for business. Heck, you already should have a couple of drop-offs written up and ready to go. And don't forget a fresh pot of coffee.

If you really want to build loyalty, don't just shove tickets in their faces when your guys get to work. Instead, take a couple of minutes to check in with them. Greet them, ask them how they're doing, and maybe take a couple of minutes for small talk about their hobbies or favorite sports teams. If this sounds a lot like the rapport-building process we discussed in the chapter on sales, that's because it is. You should be constantly building rapport with your team. It is very important to remember to do this. If you have rapport, you have their trust and this relationship with your team members allows you to ask them to give you some extra effort whenever you need it. If you take the time to build rapport, you'll never have a problem getting people to stay late now and then for a problem car or come in a little early if it looks like you're going to have a big day.

4. Train Your Technicians and Service Writers.

So you've got your team well paid and inspired. There's one piece of the puzzle left, and that's training. I have found that a simple policy for technician training works best. Your techs should be able to pursue any of the certifications they want, and as long as they pass, you should cover the classes. Remember, every bit of knowledge they gain makes them that much more valuable to you. Don't be penny-wise and pound-foolish and skimp on this high-value investment.

When it came to service writers, I created my own training class. I personally can teach your service writer how to sell service. I hope I don't sound cocky, but I'm very good at it. I've sold *something* my entire life: cars, real estate, ideas, penny stocks—you name it and I've been teaching people how to sell it for almost as long as I've been selling. Over the years, I've also successfully sold more than a million dollars in service from the front counter. I love teaching people how to improve their incomes and their lives through better selling. If you are interested in more training resources, you can find them at www.DavidDickson.com/train.

How to Successfully Confront and Correct

Now let's talk about the most difficult part of the people process: firing. Before you fire anyone, you need to be certain that you are firing the right person. You do this by setting clear standards about what is and is not acceptable. Make sure that your employees know what's expected of them, and make sure that it's measurable.

So, what if you have an employee who is falling short of a standard? How do you confront him? How do you ultimately fire him if that becomes necessary? Here's a great system that will work for you every time, if you use it the way I describe.

- When you _____

- I feel _____

- I would prefer/need _____

- (Optional) If my needs aren't met, I will _____

This is a bulletproof way to confront anybody about anything. It works as well in personal relationships as it does in business relationships. Here's an example using an employee who is consistently late for work. When he shows up late, this is what you say: "When you show up late for work, I feel angry. I need you to be on time." If he or she shows up late again, you say, "When you continue to show up late for work, I feel angry and disrespected. I need you to be on time. If you can't be on time, I will fire you." If he *still* shows up late, you say, "You're fired!"

See how simple this is? The key is to state your feelings, not your thoughts. For instance, if I said to you, "When you show up late for work, I think you're lazy," you'd probably say, "I'm not lazy!" and we'd have an argument. That's the beauty of this confrontation system. If you stick with your feelings, there is nothing to argue about. Your employee might not like to hear how you feel, but there is nothing for him or her to argue about. The other nice thing about this system is its clarity. When you use this format for confrontation, it's hard to get off track and into an argument. This is a very powerful tool. Once you've used this effective verbal confrontation system, you'll need to document whatever warning you've given. It's always best to put it in writing. More details on exactly how to fire an employee are given in the next section.

If you have a "probation period" for new employees, make sure to use it effectively. Give them opportunities to prove themselves. Use the probation period to satisfy yourself that a new employee is a good fit. In most businesses, a probation period is ninety days. However, most habits and expectations with new employees are set within the first three to five days. That's right, three to five days! This is the most important time for a new employee. It's a good idea to spend a lot of time with your new people during this period. They never will be more open to direction, and you never will have a better chance to transmit your values, vision, and goals. This is time well spent.

"You're Fired!" How to Do It Easily and Respectfully

So, you have an employee whom you've trained, inspired, coached, and confronted, and he still is not working out. How do you fire him? Let's look at this question in three parts: what you should say, where you should say it, and when you should say it.

When it's time to fire someone, the less you say the better. It's important to remember that once you say the words "You're fired!" the employee isn't going to hear anything else you have to say. When firing people, simply say, "I've called you in today to tell you that I'm letting you go. You're fired. Do you have any questions?" Usually, he or she doesn't, so wish the person good luck in the future and end the meeting. Normally, this takes less than five minutes. Do not try to explain your decision in detail. Do not make a list of all of the employee's sins (you're firing him or her, so it really doesn't matter). Do not try to give him or her career counseling. Just say the words and be done as quickly as possible.

By the time you fire someone, you should be at the end of a process of confronting and counseling. The person being fired never should be surprised. If you find that the people you are firing are shocked and surprised, you need to look at your coaching and training processes.

The next question is where you should do the firing. Your office is best. It's good to have some privacy, but if you have any concerns about violence or unpredictable reactions, have someone else join you for the firing. If you're firing someone who has been with you for a long time and is fairly emotionally predictable, you can do it alone. If you're firing someone who has been with you for a short time or seems unpredictable or likely to sue, have someone join you.

Finally, when should you do it? Let's start with when you should not do it. Never, ever fire someone when you're mad. No matter what, always take the time to calm down and make sure that you are making a business decision, not an emotional decision. Firing someone when you're angry will just lead to mistakes and legal problems.

The best time to fire someone is on Friday afternoon. This gives the person the entire weekend to absorb what's happened. By Monday, he or she will have accepted it. The person might call and ask questions about health benefits or something else, but there is normally not as much negativity.

If you owe someone a final paycheck, have it ready and

hand it to him or her when the firing takes place, even if you don't really owe it for another week or so. You also might include some sort of severance, unless the person you're firing is still on probation or has done something outrageously wrong. This makes the separation that much more final. Nothing is worse than having an ex-employee come back to pick up a final paycheck and poison your existing employees while at the shop.

The last thing about firing is the legal part. Educate yourself on your local labor laws. It's expensive and irritating to not be in compliance with these laws. However, don't ever let the fear of legal problems keep you from firing a bad employee. There is no worse reason for keeping someone who is not helping your business. Better to do the firing, take your medicine, and move on.

CHAPTER 5

Shop Flow and
Production Management

You probably feel like you have pretty good shop flow and production management processes in place right now. There might be a couple of things that you know you could do better. But hey, by definition, your system is good enough to do whatever you're doing, right? Wrong!

Shop flow and production management are the biggest holes in the bucket for most shops. And the really dangerous thing about them is their complexity. The issues are hard to identify, let alone deal with. If you look at your shop flow and production management systematically, the opportunities and necessary corrections will start to become visible.

Let's look at an effective nine-step shop flow system. Some of the steps you're probably doing already. Some of them you should be doing. Either way, this will be a profitable exercise.

Nine Steps to Easy, Profitable Shop Flow

1. Get the Customer to Enter the System.

2. Get the Customer to Go Home.

3. Diagnose the Problem.

4. Price the Job: Fast Estimates.

5. Sell the Job.

6. Shop and Order the Parts.

7. Do the Work: Monitor the Progress.

8. Verify the Repair.

9. Arrange the Pickup.

1. Get the Customer to Enter the System

The customer calls or walks in. These are the two entry points to the system. In the chapter on sales we talked about the importance of an appropriate greeting, whether in person or on the phone. If the customer is calling, the service writer sets up an appointment.

When the customer walks in, the service writer does an intake. The intake is a vital part of the shop flow process. The quality of the information gathered here will affect the repair and follow-up processes.

The key to this step is to get all of the customer's information. This includes cell phone number and email address. If the customer balks at this, simply say, "If we can't reach you once we've determined what needs to be done, we have to put you at the back of the line, which means we might not get your repair done today." That cures customers of any reluctance to give up numbers and addresses.

The customer's time constraint is another important piece of information. This needs to be explored and documented. By explored, I mean that if the customer says, "I need the car back by 2 p.m.," the service writer asks "Why?" rather than simply writing down the time. The answer tells you whether this is a hard or soft deadline. A hard deadline is a fifteen-day driving vacation along the East Coast for which the customer needs the car. A soft deadline is when the customer has to pick up Jimmy at soccer practice (you can offer a loaner or a rental).

2. Get the Customer to Go Home

Once the intake is done, customers MUST go home. This is key to profitability. "Waiters" are a lot less profitable than the people you take or send home. You can trust me on this, or you can conduct your own experiment and prove it to yourself. I've tried it both ways (letting them wait and taking them home), and the effect is verifiable and undeniable. Always take them home or to work or give them a loaner car or get them a rental or drop them off at the mall or ask them to arrange to be picked up. Do whatever you have to do to get them out of the shop.

3. Diagnose the Problem

Once the customer is gone, the service writer dispatches the ticket to a tech for diagnosis. If the intake has been done properly, there should be a pretty long and complete story for the tech to use as his starting point.

I normally give my techs ten to twenty minutes to diagnose a car. It doesn't matter what the book says; unless it's a check engine light or an electrical problem, if the tech can't tell you within twenty minutes what he thinks is wrong, then he probably won't be able to tell you, or if he does he'll probably be wrong.

Any time you doubt a diagnosis, go out into the shop and have the tech show you how he arrived at his conclusions. This does two things. First, it helps you be clear about exactly what's wrong with the car, so you can sell with confidence. The other thing it does is lets the techs know that you will be asking them to justify their diagnoses, so they better not BS you!

The tech should give his final diagnosis to your service writer *in writing.* Countless hours have been wasted and huge numbers of customers have been needlessly pissed off by technicians not putting their diagnoses in writing. This is a huge opportunity. Not putting the diagnosis in writing almost always will lead to miscommunication and wrong or incomplete repairs.

The tech should include two things in the diagnosis. First, he should have the complete cause of and correction for the problem that was stated by the customer. If you don't fix the problem he came in for, he's not gonna be happy. Trust me!

The second thing a technician should include in the diagnosis is a completed vehicle inspection form. This form should note every other repair opportunity on the vehicle that the tech has discovered. The more comprehensive and complete this form is, the more profitable the shop will be. It's just that simple. As a rule, this inspection form should be filled out for every vehicle that comes into the shop, no matter how unlikely it seems that the customer will do the work.

There isn't a single five-year-old vehicle on the road that can't use a thousand dollars' worth of repair/maintenance work. It's the tech's job to find it and document it so that the service writer can sell it.

One last point about sharing the diagnosis between the service writer and the technician: Any conversation that needs to occur should happen out in the shop. Customers waiting to drop off or pick up their cars do not need to hear any of these discussions.

4. Price the Job: Fast Estimates

Once the service writer has the diagnosis, she needs to price the job as quickly as possible. Time is of the essence.

This is a common bottleneck in most shops, and an area of great procrastination for many mediocre service writers.

If the service writer has been doing her job for more than a year, he should be able to price 75 percent of the jobs he sees just from experience and memory. If your service writer needs to go to the computer and carefully look up hours and exact parts' prices for every part on a job estimate, you should lose confidence in his ability to do his job. There is no way he'll be fast enough to handle the volume you'll need if you're to be profitable.

The important thing to remember here is that this is an *estimate*. In most shops, quick pricing is the key to doing enough volume to generate a decent profit.

When you're doing a fast estimate, you want to know how long the work is going to take.

Your techs should put the book hours on the diagnosis. If you don't know the parts' costs from experience, either call the parts house or check the computer for costs on the major parts. Next, increase each number by 5–10 percent, and then use a multiplier of between 2.5 and 4.5 on the parts, depending on the cost (the lower the cost, the higher the multiplier; there are matrixes available). This will give you a retail parts cost and a retail labor cost at book time. Add the two together and in less than three minutes (sometimes thirty seconds) you're ready to call the customer with a quote.

When you fast-price like this, you'll occasionally miss and under price a job. The key is to not get discouraged, because you'll slow the process down. You'll hit it right a hundred times more than you'll miss it, and that is what counts. The speed with which you make a quick quote will make you a lot more money than you'll ever lose on the occasional miss.

5. Sell the Job

The next step in the process is for the service writer to call and sell the repair. We covered this process very thoroughly in the chapter on selling, but let's review a few key points.

What-Why-When-How Much

At this point in the process the service writer must make sure that each of these questions is answered. They need to be answered even if the customer doesn't ask them—especially the "why" question. The best answer to the "why" is a simple unembellished version of the truth. If you know why the car broke, tell the customer in simple nontechnical terms. If you don't, say you don't. Answering this question will save you a lot of grief later.

It's also worth reviewing the closing statement: "The total cost of the repair, including parts, labor, and sales tax, is $XXX.XX. Do you have any coupons or are you a member of the Customer Care Club?"

Using this closing as presented will make you a lot of money. Deviating from it when it comes time to close the sale will cost you a lot of money. Rehearse this closing until it's a reflex.

6. Shop and Order the Parts

Once the customer agrees to the repair, the service writer shops the parts and then orders them from the lowest price source that can deliver them in a timely manner. Finding and ordering from the lowest price source is vital to your profitability. If a part costs more than $25, at least two sources should be shopped; three would be better. If the service writer has any doubt about delivery time or correctness of the part, he should order it from two sources.

Shop owners often respond to this with something like, "I don't need to shop my parts, my parts house takes care of me. And I wouldn't dream of ordering the same part from two different places. That's just not fair to the parts house." I try not to laugh when I hear this. Heck, I myself have said it before, and it's ridiculous!

The parts house is not your friend. It doesn't "take care" of you. This doesn't mean the folks there are unethical or evil; actually, they're entrepreneurs just like you. They make a profit by making as much money as you'll let them on every part they sell. Some will be incredibly fair and consistent. Others, if they can lull you to sleep and get your attention away from the prices, will club you like you're a caveman's next meal. You never know what kind you're dealing with, so you owe it to yourself and your business to be vigilant. Sure, you want to have a good relationship with your suppliers, but don't be fooled into complacency.

As for the unfairness and inconvenience to the parts house if you order the part from more than one place, it's only unfair and inconvenient for the parts house that isn't the first one there with the right part at the right price.

7. Do the Work: Monitor the Progress

Once the job is sold and the part(s) ordered, the service writer tells the tech *in writing* what work needs to be done. Nothing is worse than having a tech do every item on a ticket when the customer has agreed to pay for only a single repair. A written order eliminates this problem.

It's also very important to clearly note any time constraints on the order. The tech needs to know what kind of time he has so that he can plan his day and work this job in with all his other jobs.

In a perfect world, all this is done before 9 or 10 a.m. on most of the cars in the shop on any given day. Once all the jobs are sold and the parts ordered, the service writer needs to monitor the progress of the jobs. Have your service writer walk through the shop every thirty to forty-five minutes. If he doesn't see everything he needs to know, he should ask the tech how things are going.

Service writers have to be sensitive when checking on progress. The technicians are trained professionals, after all. Pestering them about when a car will be finished is not productive if it causes them to start cussing or throwing wrenches. This is the time for the service writer to ask, "How can I help?" The guys will know why they're there when they see them coming through the shop, and they'll usually answer the question before it is asked.

Sometimes, the tech might be stuck at the moment the service writer is checking on him. Your service writer can be most helpful if he can divide "stuck" into two categories: mental and physical. Either the tech is stuck because he can't figure something out or he's stuck because he can't get something to break loose or fit.

If the problem is mental, have your service writer try to walk through it with him. Sometimes just the extra set of eyes will reveal the answer. If the problem is physical, have the shop foreman join the discussion and give his opinion. Physical problems usually don't respond well to more force.

8. Verify the Repair

Once the tech completes the repair, he can park the car and bring his copy of the ticket back to the service writer. This next step is very important. Someone other than the tech who did the repair needs to walk out to the car and verify that whatever was done actually fixed the car. If this procedure is followed, there is absolutely no reason for a car to leave the shop not properly repaired.

If the tech fixed the A/C, start the car and make sure it's blowing nice and cold. If it was the brakes that were done, take a short ride around the block and make sure everything works properly. And do a delivery inspection. Make sure there's no grease or marks on the car, no damaged or broken trim, etc.

9. Arrange the Pickup

At this point, you can call the customer and *confirm* a 5 p.m. pickup, unless other pickup arrangements were made at drop-off. During this call you also should confirm the total cost of the repair and the acceptable methods of payment (a customer wanted to give us a cow once). Again, refer to the chapter on sales for more details about this process.

When the customer arrives, cash him out and thoroughly explain the repair (again, reference the chapter on sales). With that done, you then can set the next appointment.

Once the customer has left, it's time to initiate the follow-up sequence. Schedule the next contact and make sure that the customer is on the thank-you letter and newsletter mailing lists.

What you've just read is the most efficient and effective shop flow process. You may need to adjust it slightly in some areas because of the way your shop physically is set up, but the closer you stay to this format, the more effective and profitable your business will be.

Production Management Notes

Here are some important points about production management.

It's always best to have one person be responsible for making sure the work gets done quickly and efficiently. It can be the service writer, the shop foreman, or anyone else; it really doesn't matter. What matters is that one person has the trust and respect of the guys who are doing the work. The buck needs to stop with that person.

Profitable production relies on great systems, and great systems are implemented and maintained by great people. Every system must have a system champion. This is the person who makes it his or her responsibility to ensure that the system is working properly.

Here's an example of a simple system driven by a system champion. In my shop, we always stocked the top twenty-five oil filters. Before computerization, we needed a simple way to make sure we never ran out of those filters. My shop foreman (aka my system champion) had a simple solution. When a technician took a filter off of the shelf, he'd tear the box top off and hang it on a nail by the parts room door. Once or twice a week the shop foreman would pull the box tops off the nail and count them, call the parts house, and reorder the necessary number of filters. The shop foreman also made sure that new techs were instructed always to put their filter box tops on that nail.

This system worked because it was simple and easy to follow, and it was constantly monitored by the system champion. All the best and most effective systems are simple and easy to follow, and they all have system champions.

When it comes to production, it's important to make sure that the most profitable work comes first. Too often shops work on a first-come, first-served basis without even thinking about it. Don't make that mistake. Prioritize your jobs based on profitability. Why put a low-profit, heavy engine job ahead of a quick, highly profitable compressor replacement? Customers understand when you say, "Do you want it fast or do you want it cheap? If you can be flexible on the time, I can save you some money." Ask this of all your customers with big heavy jobs and you not only will get the jobs, you'll be able to grab the fast easy work that comes in as well.

It's also important to put your best techs on the right jobs. You don't want an A tech bogged down with a big heavy job when the bays are full of quick jobs that are easy money.

You'll suffer and so will he. Make sure that someone (your service champion) is paying attention to this as the work is being distributed.

The reason you are managing shop flow and production is to make a profit. To do that you must have effective measurements. A financial "dashboard" is the key. It's called a dashboard because you don't want to be overwhelmed with numbers. On a dashboard you have a few key numbers: speed, RPM, fuel level, and engine temperature; that's really all you need. It's the same for your shop. The most important numbers to look at on a daily basis are traffic count, Repair Order (RO) average, gross sales, and parts cost as a percentage of sales. These numbers will tell you everything you need to know about the health of your business. They also will tell you where to look if you are having problems.

If your car count is down, you need to look at your marketing. If your gross sales and RO average are down, you need to look at your service writer and sales process. If your parts cost as a percentage of sales is climbing, you're not doing a good job of shopping your parts. Each indicator on the dashboard lets you monitor and manage a critical area of your shop. If you need a simple, easy-to-use dashboard, just go to www.DavidDickson.com/benchmark.

The last item to pay attention to when looking at production management is bay utilization. The techs don't own the bays; you do. Nobody gets to "camp out" or leave a lift tied up for days. The person in charge of production needs to stay on top of this and make sure each bay is fully and properly utilized.

By the way, good bay utilization doesn't mean parking your boat or Jet Ski there. That's not a joke. I get calls all the time from shop owners who say, "I just can't do enough work to be profitable." So I'll ask the owner how many bays he has and how many techs he has. If the numbers don't add up (I prefer one per bay, but four techs for six bays is acceptable),

then I ask him to describe each bay in detail and tell me
what's there. Sure enough, seven times out of ten there's a
boat, Jet Ski, or hot rod sitting in one of the bays soaking up
profit like a big greasy sponge.

CHAPTER 6

Resources and Relationships

There are certain key business relationships that are vital to your success in an auto repair shop. We'll cover the five most important ones here.

The Five Most Important Relationships

1. Bankers
2. Accountants
3. Lawyers
4. Parts Suppliers
5. Tool Guys

1. Bankers

Let's start with the banker. How do you decide whom to use? The ideal banker for an independent auto repair shop will have several characteristics. He will have experience and a good track record of getting loans for small businesses. He also will be in the relationship banking business, not the commodity banking business. What's the difference? A relationship lender usually works in a small local bank or credit union. He makes decisions based on what he knows about the local economy and business climate. He even might hold the note locally. A large commodity lender, on the other hand, usually will work at a big national bank and is more likely to make decisions remotely based on algorithms. He probably will securitize your loan and sell it off to another bank.

In most cases, a local relationship lender will be the best fit. However, as you get bigger and need more money, you may need to move to a national bank. That is what happened to me.

The person you deal with at the bank must be able to guide you through the lending process and, hopefully, will have some influence with the decision makers. In a perfect world, you would work directly with those decision makers, but banks usually are very careful not to let this happen.

The last thing you need to know about how to choose a banker to do business with is that the bank for which he or she works has sufficient money to lend. In the past, this always was assumed, but in today's economy you never know. The best way to find out is to ask about the bank's recent lending activity. This should give you a good indication of its ability to lend.

There are four main things you need from your banker:

- Money for real estate
- Feedback on real estate decisions
- A credit line for emergency/opportunity capital
- Connections with other business service providers

You need your banker to be a source of money for real estate. Owning your own real estate is a huge business advantage. You've got to have a banker who understands your business and will work with you to make owning your own property a reality.

Along these lines, you also need feedback from your banker on real estate decisions. If you just ask for advice from your banker, unless you know her well she'll probably say something like, "I really can't advise you on whether you should buy." That's OK, because bankers will give you advice; you just have to learn to read between the lines.

If you ask for 100 percent financing on a piece of property, your banker (and bank) almost always will say no—but how they say no is important. You need to determine if they are turning you down because they're cautious about the property or because they're not sure you will be able to pay. If it's just caution, they will ask for a standard 10-20 percent down. If they're not sure you'll be able to pay, they'll ask for much more as a down payment.

If they are being cautious about the property, that's not a big deal. They're just doing their job. However, if they're looking for a down payment that is way out of proportion to the price of the property, this means that, based on the information you've given, your banker and the bank have real concerns about your ability to pay. You don't have to agree, but it is a good idea to slow down, review your decision, and make sure all the numbers add up.

The next thing you need from your bank is access to a business line of credit. When we think of this, we generally think of emergencies, but this money also is important for equipment or unique marketing opportunities. You should work with your banker to make sure that your credit line increases as your business expands.

The last thing you need from your banker is for him to be able to provide connections with other business service providers—lawyers, accountants, bookkeepers, and other professionals who are vital to the operation of a business. A good banker will know great people in all these areas and will be happy to make introductions. One bank I used held a quarterly luncheon to keep some of its best customers connected.

2. Accountants

A good accountant is critical to your success. There are two important goals you should have in mind when working with an accountant.

First, have an accurate understanding of your financial situation. With all the accounting software available today, you can do a lot of it yourself. You can input transactions at the shop level, track expenses, and even generate some reports, but a trained accountant who can review the numbers and provide important feedback always will have a much clearer picture of the financial health of your business—and will see things that you don't.

The second goal to have when working with an accountant is to pay as little in taxes as legally possible. Taxes are a huge drain on any business. It is important to spend the time and money to get professional help. The tax codes change constantly and are complex, and you shouldn't waste valuable entrepreneurial energy becoming a tax expert. This is where a good accountant is invaluable in helping you legally minimize the taxes you pay, which is the most important part of this relationship.

Also, a good accountant either will have a good bookkeeper or know of one to recommend.

3. Lawyers

There are two types of lawyers: litigators and deal makers. I have a simple rule: avoid litigators when at all possible (their job is to argue, and that's expensive) and always have a great relationship with a good deal maker.

Litigators are the kinds of lawyers who go to court. Their jobs are to argue, and the best ones are really successful at it. Unfortunately, arguing also is very expensive. It wastes time and money. Think long and hard before you hire a litigator and get into a long, expensive legal argument with someone. It will cost you a lot of money and, more important, your peace of mind. You cannot get into a big legal argument without sacrificing your serenity and happiness. Litigators are the lawyers of last resort.

Deal makers are a much better choice. They understand the high costs (in dollars and serenity) of arguing. They pride themselves on rarely if ever seeing the inside of a courtroom. Instead of going to trial, they find ways to compromise and deal with people their clients have disagreements with. They find ways to avoid litigation. A good relationship with a great deal-making lawyer will be one of the best investments you make in your success.

4. Parts Suppliers

Parts suppliers are another vital business relationship to have. The first rule with parts suppliers is never to use just one. Lack of competition breeds complacency on both sides of the relationship. It's not that they're evil; it's just that sometimes, if they don't have to compete, they'll take your business for granted. In addition, delivery times invariably suffer when you deal with only one parts house. Since they know they don't have to compete for your business, you're just not as high a priority as the guy down the street who is using more than one parts source.

Another problem is that when you use only one parts supplier, its employees and your employees get too familiar; parts for your tech's hot rod "accidentally" end up on your parts bill (I'll tell you how to prevent this in a minute), or parts drivers hang out and chat with your technicians when the techs should be working. None of these things help your profitability.

Finally, when you only have one parts supplier, you have no leverage when it comes to returns or labor claims. The parts house isn't worried that you're going to take your business elsewhere, because it knows that you have no other relationships with other parts suppliers.

So, how do you get the best discount with your suppliers? As I mentioned, always have at least two, preferably three, primary parts suppliers. As your company expands, you should be using five or six at any given time. Remember, these guys live and die by the business they get from you, so make them earn it.

The next step to getting big discounts is always to shop around. If the part costs more than $25, shop for it with at least two suppliers; the more the better. You'll be amazed at how much prices vary for the same parts. Compare the big chains to the small locals, and don't forget the dealerships. Sometimes they will surprise you with how inexpensive they can be.

Always know roughly what your weekly parts expenditure is. This is a great number to throw around when shopping. For instance, tell a potential supplier, "I spend $10,000 a week on parts. If you can give me great prices and short delivery times, a big piece of that could be yours."

Don't be afraid to let the parts houses know that you are shopping them. They probably know already, but you never should miss a chance to remind them. You don't get to keep your customers unless you have the best deals. The same should apply to your parts suppliers keeping you.

Here's why it's so important to do a good job managing your parts supplier relationships: It's the easiest money you'll ever make. Let me explain. If you sell a $500 job, you might make $100-$200 net after expenses, depending on your costs. However, if you save a dollar on parts, you've just made a dollar. If you know your numbers, you'll know that every dollar you save in parts is like selling $5 at the front counter. This adds up to serious money fast. Focus a little attention on this area and watch your profits grow.

I have clients who connect their service writers' pay to the cost of parts. For instance, the service writer will get 6 percent of the parts and labor if the parts cost is 30 percent or higher, and 8 percent if the parts cost comes down to 23 percent. There is usually a sliding scale from 6-8 percent. This is a great way to get service writers focused on profit opportunities that frequently are overlooked in many shops.

Parts Returns

Another thing you need to pay attention to in your relationships with parts suppliers is returns. Too many times, shop owners put themselves out of business by not paying attention to the returns process. Here are a few key tips.

Always have one place in the shop where returns go. That way you, your service writer, your technicians, and the parts drivers all know where to look. Always make sure to get paperwork on every return. Don't ever accept "I'm busy; I'll bring the paperwork back to you later" from a parts driver. Too often they "just didn't get around to it" and you end up with a charge and no part, and they end up with a free part to sell.

Along the same lines, make sure every part ties to a repair order. Have a standing rule with your parts houses: If the invoice doesn't have a valid RO number from you on it, you're not going to pay for the part. Your service writers and all the parts suppliers need to understand how important this is. Reconcile the tickets every day. It only should take a few minutes. This is what keeps employees from ordering parts under your account for their personal vehicles or for side work at home. This one rule will protect you from one of the biggest sources of shrinkage (another word for theft) in the auto repair business.

5. Tool Guys

For long periods of time, I've let no tool guys on my property. During those periods, my business thrived and expanded. At their best, tool guys can help you out of a jam with special tools or referrals to great technicians. I've actually met two who did this consistently (thanks, Reggie and Bill). The rest, however, just wasted my guys' time with unproductive gossip about other shops or, even worse, tried to recruit them for those shops.

Based on these experiences, I've come up with a set of guidelines that will allow you to successfully manage your relationships with the tool guys. Limit them to 15-minute visits when they stop in. Fifteen minutes doesn't sound like much, but think about it this way: If you have four techs and they all stop for 15 minutes to go hang out at the tool truck, you've just lost one hour of production time *that you'll never get back.* This gets expensive real fast!

Also, allow only two tool trucks to service your shop. For a while, it seemed like every retired technician was getting his own tool franchise. It just gets to be too unprofitable and ridiculous to let them all come in. The guys may not like it at first, but they will understand. Even the tool drivers will appreciate it once they understand the rules.

CHAPTER 7

Fatal Mistakes
and Attitudes

Over the years of growing my business from one small auto repair shop to twenty-one profitable shops, I've watched a lot of shop owners and managers struggle. Some have succeeded and some have failed. The ones who failed usually did so because they made what I call fatal mistakes. These are mistakes in attitude or action that destroyed them either by putting them out of business or getting them fired. Here are six fatal attitudes that will get you every time.

1. Greed

There is a difference between being profit focused and being greedy. Being profit focused is necessary to running a business; it guarantees that you and everyone you work with will make money. On the other hand, being greedy means considering only yourself while disregarding the needs of the people you do business with.

When you're profit focused, you think long term, making deals and doing business in ways that give everyone around you the opportunity to profit.

If you're greedy, you think short term and selfishly take advantage of the people you work with, not thinking about them or the long-term future.

If you build your business based on profit, you might start off a little slower, but you'll quickly create a team and build lots of momentum. If you are greedy, you may fool some people at the start, but they'll quickly realize that you're only looking out for yourself. Greedy behavior is hard to sustain. You alienate a lot of people, and it gets harder and harder to attract colleagues.

The key to avoiding the corrosive effects of greed on your business is to recognize that you are building something long term and sustainable. Another important point to remember is that greed-driven businesses usually are hard to sell, whereas profit-driven businesses are very attractive to buyers.

I knew a greedy shop owner who thought he was being smart and effective. Everything was about feeding his greed. In every deal he had to get more, more, more, without thinking about how this would affect his partners or the other people in the deal. He thought his employees loved him and were loyal. Actually, they hated him and stole from him whenever they got the chance. For a while his business grew, but eventually all his quality people went to work for other repair shops. His reputation for being greedy was so bad that he no longer could maintain his business. There is a high price to pay for being greedy.

On the other hand, there are great rewards for focusing on profits. It's fun being around profit-focused shop owners. They attract great people, everyone makes a lot of money, and they have fun doing it. These types of shop owners know they're working to make a profit, and they have no problem sharing, because they understand the incredible power of a profit-focused team.

If you find yourself focused on making money only for yourself, stop for a minute and remember what motivational speaker Zig Ziglar said: "You can have everything in life you want, if you will just help other people get what they want."

2. Being Inflexible

The next fatal attitude is inflexibility. You must be able to roll with the punches and remain flexible when seeking solutions to the problems you face as you build your business. A key to being an effective problem solver is to accept new ideas and turn them into creative actions. If you're inflexible, you won't be able to do this.

You can stick with your old ideas when it's appropriate, but when faced with a problem or challenge in the shop, make sure to look at every possible solution, no matter how radical it may seem to you. When I opened my first shop, one reason I was able to create so much success so quickly was because I didn't know what I couldn't do. I wasn't limited by inflexible thinking, like most of my employees and competitors were. Try forgetting all the rules and see what happens.

It's a simple fact: The more rigid you are, the more likely you are to fail! The auto repair business is dynamic and constantly changing. If you can't change, you can't keep up. The types of cars and the profit opportunities we had five years ago are gone. They've been replaced by a whole new set of challenges and opportunities. If you're not flexible, you'll be left behind.

Here's a quick method to help you bring flexibility to your problem-solving process at the shop. First, identify the problem. Make sure you know what you are trying to fix. Since you do this with cars all day long, this should be easy. However, sometimes familiarity makes us lazy, and you might find yourself jumping past this step. When in doubt, take the time to write down your understanding of the problem.

Once you've clearly identified the problem, the next step is to come up with possible solutions. You are not taking action yet, just thinking about different ways you could solve the problem. This is where flexibility is useful. Once you've looked at all the obvious answers, look a little harder and see if you can find some that are not so obvious.

Here's an example: I was having trouble getting rebuilt A/C compressors that actually worked. I tried one parts supplier after another, with the same results. I was getting very frustrated, and then a friend suggested that I open my own compressor rebuilding business. Wow! I hadn't thought of that, but I was willing to be flexible and explore the idea. Once I thought it through, I decided it actually could work. I ended up with a fantastically profitable new business and great compressors that almost always work—a victory for flexible, nonrigid thinking.

Taking action and monitoring are the last two steps of the flexible problem-solving process. Once you've settled on and started a course of action, monitor the situation carefully to make sure that what you're doing is actually solving the problem. If it is, great! Keep moving full speed ahead. If it's not, stop and review your decision and either make adjustments or abandon that solution and try a different one.

Without getting too deeply into psychology, there are a couple of important things to understand about the way we look at problems and solutions that can lead to inflexible thinking.

The first is "confirmation bias," also known as tunnel vision. It means that once we get an idea, the only information we pay attention to is information that supports that idea. We tend to ignore any information that might challenge it. The key to getting past this is to have an open mind and people around you who can offer different points of view and alternative ideas. Of course, the people around you have to be comfortable and willing to share, and you have to be open and willing to listen. This is why it's so important to have good relationships with all your employees. When there is a problem with production or the flow of work through the shop and you find yourself at a loss for ideas, you always should get your technicians and service writer involved. They almost always can come up with solutions that just might be more creative and effective than yours would be.

Another important thought process that leads to inflexibility is "insufficient hypothesis." In English, this means jumping on the first solution that comes to mind without exploring other options. I'm a very action-oriented guy, so this is something I have to be very careful about. The key to overcoming this inflexibility trap is to slow down and look at two or three possible solutions for every problem you face, rather than jump on the first one. If you get in the habit of doing this, you'll find yourself coming up with much better solutions without delaying your actions much at all.

To be successful in auto repair, you have to make flexible problem solving natural and instinctive. The more open-minded and willing to question your assumptions you are, the more likely it is that you will find profitable, creative solutions to the challenges you face. Ask lots of questions and think carefully before taking action.

3. Being Angry All the Time

The next fatal attitude is chronic anger. This isn't the same as getting mad about particular issues. Being chronically angry means being pissed off all the time about everything.

The problem with this attitude is that, just like greed, it chases people away. If you are always angry, eventually no one is going to want to be around you. When the people around you leave, all their great ideas and skills go with them.

So what do you do if you think you're guilty of chronic anger? Simple. Get some help. Usually, this isn't something you can fix yourself. It requires new ideas and different views of the problem. I hate to sound cliché, but an anger management class might be a good place to start. People who attend these classes learn a set of concrete skills for dealing with their anger that absolutely can change their lives.

The point here isn't to avoid anger completely. There are times when anger is appropriate and can be channeled to increase your performance. The key is to make sure that your anger is working for you, not against you. If you have any doubts or are concerned that you make the fatal mistake of being chronically angry, do yourself, your business, and the people you work with a big favor and get some help.

4. Getting Frustrated or Impatient

The next fatal attitude I often see is frustration or impatience. Too many times, someone opens a shop and then gets frustrated because he isn't wealthy and retired in six months.

Opening a shop is not like winning the lottery. It takes time and effort. My life is great right now. I have the luxury of total control over my time, and frankly, I usually don't work very hard. The rest of the story is that I worked my butt off for the first four or so years. I was in the shop at 6:30 in the morning and I rarely left before 7 at night. If I had gotten frustrated or impatient at the beginning, I wouldn't be where I am today.

If you're susceptible to frustration or impatience, you must learn how to deal with it. The best method is to have a positive attitude and clear goals. If you keep yourself positive by surrounding yourself with positive people and filling your mind with positive messages, you're much less likely to get frustrated. If you still get frustrated, then all you have to do is revisit your goals and remind yourself that even though the present situation might be frustrating, you're moving steadily toward what you really want—a successful business of your own.

Freedom and control of your time should be among your key goals. If you achieve these, you will be wealthy in more ways than just monetarily. As you grow the business, you might occasionally hire a key employee who you think will allow you freedom, and for a time you'll have some, but then the employee fails and you're right back in the middle of things. Very frustrating. When this happens, just remind yourself that it worked for a little while and there was no problem with your goal; you just need to keep searching for the right people to help you achieve that goal.

5. Ignoring Problems

Another fatal attitude is ignoring problems. Ignoring problems does not make them go away. Ignored problems just get bigger.

I've had shops where I knew I had an unprofitable manager at one time or another. Instead of dealing with the problem as I became aware of it, I looked the other way and hoped it would improve by itself. It didn't. Each time, the problem just continued to drain profit from my business until I finally had to do something about it. If you discover a similar problem and can address it when it's small, inexpensive, and manageable, do it.

Sometimes part of the problem is identifying it while it's still small. This is where the dashboard we talked about earlier plays a vital role. Once you see an indicator on your financial dashboard begin to stray from its "normal" reading, take quick corrective action to prevent more-severe problems from arising.

6. Lack of Persistence

The final fatal attitude is lack of persistence. If you run a business (or are trying to be successful at anything) and are willing to always accept no for an answer, you will fail.

As every successful salesperson knows, you don't give up on a sale until you've gotten at least five nos. The same is true when running a business. You can't let yourself be stopped at the first negative response.

This is particularly important to remember when dealing with government bureaucracy. They always say no the first time. It's their job. They could care less whether you succeed or fail. They have to follow a set of rules. The good news is that the rules are open to interpretation. If you don't like the answer you get the first time, just ask the question a different way or of a different person. Persistence will pay off.

Another key to overcoming lack of persistence is to ask the people or institutions that are stopping you to help you instead. For instance, when I went looking for a loan to buy my first piece of property, I had to go to eleven different banks before I found one that would lend me the money I needed. When a bank turned me down, instead of getting angry and frustrated I became persistent. The person turning me down was usually uncomfortable with having to do it. He or she had done this before and knew that people usually get righteous and angry when they hear the news that they've been turned down. So instead, I simply thanked the person for looking at my application and asked one powerful question: "Do you know of anyone who might be able to help me?"

The person would then spit out two or three names of other banks and people I should talk to. People in this position were so relieved that I wasn't mad at them that they were willing to give me their very best resources. I just followed the trail until I found a bank that could help me. If I had lacked persistence and stopped asking, I never would have gotten the first loan and never would have been able to begin building my business. I would not have what I have today.

Lack of persistence is a dangerous mistake if you are trying to grow your business.

Fatal Attitudes—Final Thoughts

Fatal attitudes are poison. They cause you either to fail to take action or to take the wrong action. Either way, the results can be devastating to you and your business.

One of the best antidotes to fatal attitudes is to surround yourself with positive messages and feedback from motivators like Dale Carnegie, Napoleon Hill, Zig Ziglar, and so many others. These people and those like them deliver constant streams of powerful, positive, life-giving, business-building messages. If you haven't read any of their work, you owe it to yourself to start today. If you have, then it's never a bad time to go back and read them again.

Constant vigilance and positive action are your best protection against the dangerous poison of fatal attitudes.

CHAPTER 8

Fatal Mistakes – Actions
and Non-Actions

We've talked about fatal attitudes that can hurt your business. Now let's talk about fatal actions. These involve either doing the wrong things or not doing the right things. Here are six fatal actions to avoid.

1. Not Paying Yourself

The first fatal action is not paying yourself. You always should get paid; that's why you go to work. Always pay yourself something, even if you're nearly broke. Sometimes it might be only $100 a week, but it's an important token and an acknowledgment that you are doing something valuable and deserve to be paid for it.

Too many times auto repair shop owners give up *all* their income when the shop is in crisis. While this is understandable, it's also dangerous. The danger is that you might begin to resent the business. An owner who is not giving himself a paycheck begins to look at his business as the enemy. He resents it because it robs him of all his time and he's getting *nothing* in return. Receiving a paycheck, no matter how small it is, can prevent this from happening.

Another important reason to pay yourself is that your paycheck becomes a scorecard. The amount you are able to take home each week (or however often you choose to do so) usually goes up and down; it rarely ever stays the same. If it's going up, you know you are doing a great job running the business. If it's going down, you know you need to make some changes. You are the ultimate "pay for performance" employee. You need this feedback.

It's also important for all your employees to understand the math. Once you know what you want to make, you can figure out what the business has to bring in so you can make that much. Once you know that number, you'll have a clear picture of what you need each team member to produce. From there, you need to work with your team to turn those numbers into actionable goals and make sure they have all the resources they need to achieve them. All this flows directly from making sure you give yourself a paycheck. Not paying yourself can be a fatal mistake.

2. Not Going to Work

The next fatal action is sort of a non-action: not going to work. Usually, this happens when someone starts to have a little success. He has worked hard and it is finally starting to pay off, so he starts to come in a little later and leave a little earlier. Before you know it, he isn't coming in at all.

When an owner or leader stops showing up at work, a couple of things result, usually in a particular order. First, morale suffers. The employees feel neglected and abandoned. As soon as these feelings set in, all systems begin to break down. They don't all just stop working at once; they gradually become less consistent and less effective. And as systems deteriorate, profits evaporate.

One of the primary reasons for building a business is so you can leave it alone and let it produce money with very little effort on your part. So the *goal* of not having to go to work is a good one. The key is in how it's executed. You have to build a team of leaders before you can step away. You have to teach them, coach them, and constantly encourage them. You have to give them the chance to practice leading the business on their own, with you close by to help out in case there's a problem. You can't just abruptly stop going to work. That will fail every time.

3. Not Constantly Learning

Another fatal non-action is not constantly learning. This is very similar to the attitude of inflexibility but is a lot more concrete.

To be successful, you must keep educating yourself. You have to study your market, your competitors, and your business. You have to be willing to bring in resources and knowledge to move your business forward. You have to be systematic and relentless about it.

I had grown my business from one store to five, and we still were writing all our invoices by hand. This had to change. We had to implement some kind of computer system, but I didn't know how.

So I educated myself. I hired a consultant and over the next six months spent more than $50,000 and countless hours studying different shop management and point-of-sale systems. I reviewed forty, tried out twelve, and actually went out and visited shops that were using the top five. I narrowed those five down to two. I got proposals from both of those companies and ultimately chose the one that I still use today.

Education isn't cheap, but it ultimately isn't expensive either. If you make an investment in learning, it will pay dividends forever. If you are not constantly, regularly making this kind of investment, you'll fall behind and eventually fail.

Back before computer mapping software was inexpensive and readily available, I spent $10,000 to have a company map out the locations of all my customers in relation to my shop. I learned some things about the value of certain neighborhoods and areas around my business that my competitors didn't know. Within a year, three of my closest competitors were out of business and my business was thriving. Coincidence or consequence? I say consequence. It is very risky and even can be fatal to not keep educating yourself and be constantly learning.

4. Hiring Relatives

Another fatal action is hiring relatives. This is not a popular thing to say, because it never fails that a small shop will hire a relative or two. So here is a modified version of the statement: The fatal action is hiring relatives with the belief that they are the best people for the job.

The key here is to not lie to yourself. The odds that your mother, brother, sister, uncle, or wife will be the *best* person for a particular job in your shop is about the same as your odds of winning the lottery. It's just not rational, yet time after time shop owners fool themselves into believing it is a good idea.

This is an important point. It's OK to hire a relative, just be clear that you are helping your family while making a business compromise. If your family depends on the business income (which it probably does), then you need to be extra careful. You need to understand all the risks.

What if the relative doesn't work out? Who confronts him or her? Who holds the person accountable? Who does the firing? What happens to family relationships if you do have to fire a relative? I bet it would make Christmas at Grandma's house a lot more interesting. All these questions need to be considered before you hire a relative.

Another thing to remember about hiring relatives is that they will be *in* your business. They will know all the details of every success and failure. And from my experience, they often will be resentful when you succeed and joyful when you fail. It doesn't seem to make sense, but it happens time after time. When I speak to auto repair shop owners, I often ask who works the hardest *against* them. The answer almost always is the employed relative.

Hiring relatives *can* work, but you must be honest with yourself if you are going to do it successfully. The fatal flaw is not being honest with yourself about the challenges associated with hiring members of your family.

5. Spending Carelessly or Foolishly

The next fatal action is spending carelessly or foolishly. I like to scuba dive. When you are underwater, the only air you have is the air in your tank. You constantly are monitoring your air. You are very careful not to use too much when you exert yourself, because you've got a limited amount to work with.

This analogy applies pretty well to your business. At any given time, you have a limited amount of money to work with. How well you handle that money determines whether you survive.

The key is to conserve your cash while making smart long-term decisions. Too many times, small-shop owners spend all their cash reserves on one piece of equipment that some salesman promised them would produce fantastic profits. Usually, it doesn't work out quite the way the salesman promised.

Heck, we all have a machine sitting somewhere in the shop that we were sure was going to be the next big thing. It's important not to bet the entire farm and all your cash reserves on something like this. That is careless. Better to lease the machine for a limited time until it proves its worth.

In a small business, cash flow is everything. You can be wildly profitable on paper, but if you don't have good cash flow, you'll be shut down before you know it. Spending carefully is an important way to control cash.

We've talked about spending carelessly; now let's talk about spending foolishly. Oftentimes shop owners who start to make a little money immediately go out and buy boats, new houses, Jet Skis, all-terrain vehicles, fancy cars, and other kinds of expensive distractions.

It's not that you shouldn't reward yourself. It's a great idea to have fun, buy "toys," and make your life better, but the business has got to be on a rock-solid foundation before you can start doing these things.

6. Not Meeting the Needs of Your Partners and Employees

The final fatal action is not meeting the needs of partners and employees. Your partners and employees are the most important people in your business. In most cases, without them you don't have a business. They aren't involved with you for the sheer joy of being around you. They're there because they want something out of the business, just as you do. You need to find out what that something is and help them get it, whether it's money, power, notoriety, acknowledgement, or any number of things. You can't take these people for granted, because if you do, they'll leave. You must find out what motivates them and what they want out of the business.

The best way to do this is to ask. One of the best partnerships I ever had started with me asking my potential partner what he wanted. When he told me, I couldn't believe it. It was so easy. He wanted to retire without getting completely out of the business. I wanted a business that would grow. It was the perfect arrangement. We both got exactly what we wanted. Throughout the partnership I made sure that he never had to work, and he gave me great guidance on building the business. It worked because we each made sure the other's needs got met.

When working with partners and employees, it's very important not to surprise them. If there is something you want or need out of the business, you must clearly explain what's in it for them and how you intend to proceed. If you fail to do this, they will feel blindsided. If you want to take the business in a different direction, make sure you have a good reason for doing so. Give your partners and employees plenty of time to ask questions and become comfortable with your intended course of action.

Partners need recognition. Many times just a heartfelt "thank you" will do. If the business is making money, then the partner usually will be satisfied. If not, then there probably is work to be done on the business and the relationship.

Employees also need recognition. The most important form of recognition for them is pay. Make sure they are paid well when they perform. After that, they want to know they are appreciated. It's important to find fun and creative ways to show this appreciation.

I once had a great technician who was a NASCAR fan. He had been with me for a while and was doing a fantastic job. I wanted to show my appreciation. I had won a contest and received VIP tickets to the Daytona 500. I gave them to him to show my appreciation. It was one of the happiest days of his life; he talked about it for years afterward.

Failing to recognize your partners and employees is a fatal mistake. Avoid it by meeting their needs and giving them the recognition   and   acknowledgment   they   deserve.

Fatal Actions—Final Thoughts

All your results come directly from your actions, either the actions you take or the actions you fail to take. As you grow your business and develop your own slingshot experience, always remember that action is the key. Also remember that when you're in doubt, it's almost always better to act. If you make a mistake, you usually can go back and fix it. If you miss an opportunity, you can't go back and make that opportunity present itself again.

CHAPTER 9

Time – The Key to Profitability

You know time is important. You hear about it everywhere. Procrastination and inefficiency are the enemies of profit. All you need to make more money are some tools to help you handle time more efficiently. In this chapter you'll learn seven tools to help you get more out of your time. But first …

Why Time Is Important

Let's start by defining why time is so important. More cars break down in your area every day than you possibly can fix at your shop. This is a great thing to remember. If you could get even a small fraction of those cars to come to your shop, you would be overwhelmed with business (I presented how to do this in the chapter on marketing). One of the main factors limiting how much work you can do is time.

Efficiency (the ability to manage time) marks the difference between good performance and great performance. It's the difference between making money and losing money.

Time is your only nonrenewable resource. If your building burns down, you can build a new one; if your employees quit, you can hire new ones; if you lose some money, you can make more. But if you lose time, you never can get it back. This makes time a very precious resource. So how do you capture more of it and use it more effectively? Here are the seven keys.

1. The Clock in Your Head

First, you must have an internal clock in your head. When you give a ticket to a technician for diagnosis, the clock starts running. If you haven't seen him in fifteen or twenty minutes, then you need to go find him. You need to check in and see how he's doing and whether he's stuck making the proper diagnosis.

When you give a technician a repair order, the clock starts running. Every thirty to forty-five minutes, make sure to walk out into the shop and see if his progress matches the clock in your head.

When you order a part, the clock starts running. If the part isn't at the shop when the clock tells you it should be, get on the phone to the parts house and track it down.

All the important things that happen in the shop every day should be tracked by the clock in your head. If you don't have this internal clock, start developing one by using your watch or the clock on the wall. You'll be amazed at how quickly you can develop this vital time management skill.

2. The "Push"

The next tool for time management in the shop is the "push." You have to constantly remind everyone on your team how important time is—without making them crazy or angry. It's a balancing act. When in doubt, you should err on the side of pushing too much. They might get a little irritated in the moment, but at the end of the week, when they see their big paychecks, they always will be grateful for the push.

The best way to push simply is to walk around and ask questions. "When will it be ready?" "Do you have everything you need?" "Is there any way I can help?" Sometimes the answer will be "Just leave me alone and let me work," but that's OK. By going out into the shop and just asking these simple questions you keep everyone focused. You also eliminate the opportunity for anyone to hide. Learn to push by practicing. You'll discover that your people can do amazing things with the right amount of "pushing."

3. Emptying the Shop Every Day

Another key to capturing more time and profit is to empty the shop every day. It's amazing how many times a shop owner or service writer will say, "I like to have a couple of jobs held over so that we've got something to start with the next day." This is wrong, wrong, wrong! To maximize your profits, you've got to push to deliver every car every day. Occasionally, a car might have to spend the night because of a parts problem, but 95 percent of the time you should be doing one-day service jobs. If you look at your profits, you'll see that in most cases, if a car spends more than one night in your shop, your profit will be way below acceptable. You must empty the bays tonight to make room for tomorrow's profits.

If you are doing your marketing, sales, and follow-up procedures correctly, you won't have empty bays in the morning, because you will have six to eight cars on the schedule every day.

4. Knowing When to Do Oil Changes

Another thing that will help you manage your time more efficiently is to schedule oil changes for first thing in the morning. If you have two techs, schedule two oil changes. If you have six techs, schedule six oil changes. The techs will know that before they do any "real" work they each probably will have at least one oil change to knock out. Of course, if they fill out complete inspection forms for these oil changes, 40 percent should turn into "real" work. The key is to not do oil changes at any other time of the day. Think about it: You generally lose money or break even on oil changes anyway. They are not a profit center; they are a "loss leader" (a marketing tool) designed to get people to come in or come back. That means that you do them at your convenience, not the customer's. Nothing destroys good production time management faster than a couple of unexpected, unprofitable oil changes in the middle of the day. It also doesn't do much for your techs' morale.

5. Blocking and Chunking

Blocking and chunking is another great way to get more productivity out of the time you have each day. If you have to make a phone call, wait until you have several calls to make and do them all at once. If you need to have a couple of meetings, schedule them for the same day, in the same place, if possible. If you have to run personal errands, try to do them all at the same time. Simple things like grouping similar activities together will result in incredible gains in time management.

6. Being Responsible for Protecting Your Time

As a shop owner, you have a lot of responsibility. And if you're not careful, many people will claim some of your time every day until you suddenly have no time left for important strategic decisions. Instead, you will be in react mode all the time, moving from one crisis to the next. It's very important to have certain times every day when you turn off your cell phone and don't take calls. Just because it rings doesn't mean you have to answer it. Tell people you will be available by phone only at certain times of the day. Train them rather than fall back on them training you. Shut the door to your office or, even better, don't go into the office first thing every morning. Learn to say "no" or "yes, but ..." If somebody asks for something that will take too much of your time, simply say no. If it fits into your agenda, say yes, but make clear how much time or effort you can devote to that particular request. For instance, a mechanic asks you to help him put an evaporator in a car he's working on, and you know it's not the best use of your time. So you simply say, "No, I don't have time to assist you, but I can take a quick look and recommend the best way to do it." Also, stop people when they try to tell you too much. Say something like, "I don't want to be rude, but you are giving me way too much information. What do you really need from me?" Most of the time, the person is looking for help making a decision. Oftentimes it's not necessary to have all the information before helping make that decision.

7. Delegating

The final step in managing time for profitability is to delegate. Do your job (which is, ideally, setting the vision and strategic goals for the business) and let your employees do theirs (getting the work done to achieve those goals). Enjoy knowing that people are making money for you while you are at the beach or in the mountains or spending time with your family. This is probably one of the hardest time tools to get independent repair shop owners to use. Most shop owners need a lot of coaching and practice to get over the guilt they feel about delegating.

Here's a story to put things in perspective. When I was a young pup in the auto business, I would to try to impress my boss by working eighty-plus hours a week and doing everything myself. He called me into the office one day and said, "I'm not impressed. Lack of delegation shows lack of trust and leadership. Do you want to be a worker or a leader?" Wow! That straightened me out very quickly. I can't say I changed overnight, but it certainly got my attention, and I set a goal to delegate more and work less. Within a year I was general manager of the dealership. He gave me the greatest secret there is for time management: Expand your reach and your efficiency by getting other people to do things for you.

The steps to effective delegation really are quite simple. Tell people WHAT you want done. Define the task clearly. Paint a picture of what it should look like when it's done. Be very specific. Write it down if it takes more than two sentences to explain.

Tell them WHEN it needs to be done. Set a firm deadline. Get a commitment from them. Make sure they understand and agree.

Tell them HOW to do it. Tell them what resources are available. Again, if it takes more than two sentences, put it in writing. This really is just external goal setting (which I'll talk more about in a later chapter). Here's an example of a delegation statement:

"I expect you to generate an additional $500 a day in gross profit. I expect this increase to occur by next week. I expect you to do it by selling more service items, specifically fuel induction services and transmission flushes. I don't expect any customer satisfaction problems resulting from this increased sales pressure. Does this seem reasonable to you? Do you have any questions?" If the person agrees, great; if he doesn't, find out why and what he needs from you to successfully complete the task. Always make sure to reach an agreement!

If you follow these steps and somebody fails to accomplish a task, you can assume that the person either DOESN'T

KNOW or DOESN'T CARE. If he doesn't know, get him more training. If he doesn't care, get rid of him! Have you ever been given a task and then been abandoned? How did it feel? Don't do this to anyone. Delegate, don't abandon. Always be available. Check in frequently and let the person know that you are available to answer any questions or provide assistance with any problems that might come up. If you are not available for some reason, make sure someone else is. Loneliness is the worst feeling of all. Most of the time, when people have trouble delegating, it's because they're actually abandoning.

People really want to help. Your employees want to feel useful and responsible. They want to feel like adults, not children. Give them your trust. Delegate and watch your business grow.

Time Warp

In science fiction, the concept of a time warp (which gives you the ability to move forward or backward in time) is a favorite subject. It's popular because the idea of controlling time is appealing, since most people feel so out of control when it comes to this aspect of their lives. If you can apply the suggestions in this chapter, you'll be in a powerful minority, the group of people who feel very comfortable with and in control of their time. That is a great group to be part of.

CHAPTER 10

The Best Way for You to Grow

Because I grew rapidly from one small auto repair shop into a profitable twenty-one-shop chain, shop owners regularly consult me about the growth of their businesses. They usually come to me saying something like, "Dave, I want to add more shops. How do I do it?" Or "Dave, there is a guy a couple of miles from me going out of business and I want to buy his shop. How do I do it?"

Why Do You Want to Grow? A Reality Check

We'll get to the answers to the above questions in a minute, but let's start with another question: "Why?!" In the last chapter of this book we'll talk about goal setting and how personally damaging the attitude of more, more, more can be. In this section, however, we'll talk about that attitude in relation to the actual business.

First, a reality check.

If you think it'll be easy to open a second or a third shop, you're wrong. It doesn't get easy until the fifth or sixth one, and even then it's not really *easy;* you just encounter a whole different set of problems.

Opening a new shop will not immediately increase the size of your bank account. If you do it really well, you'll get a little more money now and a lot more money sometime much later. If you don't do it well, it will cost you a lot of money now. You'll be fighting for your life all over again—just like you did when you opened your first shop.

If you believe a new shop will give you more free time, you're delusional. Go see a shrink. Opening a new shop is like having a baby. It may be cute, but it will be the most demanding and expensive little critter you've ever had to care for.

OK, so you've read my reality check and you're still interested in opening another shop. Congratulations! You are unquestionably an honest-to-goodness, real live entrepreneur. As such, you need to consider some additional facts about the growth process.

Three Ways to Grow without Opening Additional Shops

1. Own the Property under Your Existing Shop
2. Maximize Your Existing Shop
3. Evaluate Your Overhead

1. Own the Property under Your Existing Shop

Here is an important rule: Ultimately, you should own the property under your shop, even if you have to rent it when you start out or expand. Your property either should be inexpensive or in a high-traffic area, and preferably the latter. If your property is both of these things, congratulations.

Ownership of the property is critical for two reasons. First, it allows you to control your destiny. No one can terminate your lease and kick you out. Second, as a property owner you are building equity in a valuable asset. This will be an important part of your exit strategy down the road. Ideally, you should accomplish property ownership in your existing shop before you think about expanding.

2. Maximize Your Existing Shop

If you have one really profitable shop, make sure you've maximized it before you consider opening another one. I started with a six-bay shop. I quickly filled it up. So I added awnings out back to accommodate six more cars. I quickly filled them up. So I rented the eight-bay building next door. When I had all fourteen bays and the six awnings out back full most of the time, I started looking at other shops. The money I made by maximizing my first shop allowed me to grow easily and quickly. If I had tried to grow too soon, I would have been lacking the resources (money and/or people) necessary to grow.

Look at your existing shop. Where can you add? What about adjacent properties? What about changing the flow? What about moving the Jet Ski or hot rod to your personal garage? Figure out how can you improve and maximize the potential of your existing shop *before* you jump into a second shop. It'll be a lot quicker, easier, and less expensive than opening a new shop.

3. Evaluate Your Overhead

As you make the decision to grow, consider a few more things. When you grow, everything gets bigger. Your overhead goes up, so you have to be more productive. You have more employees and all their potential for work—and potential to give you headaches.

You also become a much bigger target for government regulation and enforcement, especially when budgets are tight. This is particularly true if your locations are spread throughout different cities and counties; each city and county has its own set of rules that you must follow. So the biggest question you have to answer at this point is: Will opening another shop improve the quality of your life (in terms of time, money, power, prestige, and anything else you can think of) enough to make it worth the investment and the risk? If the answer is yes, keep reading.

Six Keys to Growing Successfully with Multiple Shops

1. Understand Your New Role

2. Make Sure You Have the Cash

3. Pick a Location and Negotiate Your Best Deal

4. Find the Best People

5. Open for Business

6. Don't Waste Time and Money on a "Grand Opening" Day

1. Understand Your New Role

Let's talk about one of the biggest challenges you'll face when opening a new shop: you. In one shop, even if you delegate a lot, you still can walk out and touch everything. If the shop is having a slow day, you know it immediately; you can see it and feel it. If one of your people is having a problem, you can deal with it on the spot. In short, if something needs to be fixed, you are right there to fix it. You easily can manage the regular flow of business and any surprises that pop up.

When you open another shop, you'll need to take on a completely different role. You no longer can handle everything by yourself. You'll need to create systems and have them manned by good people, people who can identify and deal with everything from the regular flow of business to the unusual and the unexpected. You may be saying to yourself, "Yeah, but they all will have my cell phone number, so it shouldn't be a problem." Bad assumption. Just because they have your cell number doesn't mean they'll call you at exactly the right time and ask you exactly the right question to avoid a huge problem.

A football analogy explains this best. When you first open your business you're like the team's quarterback, leading from the front lines, right in the middle of the action. If you do the right things and have some success, you move from being the quarterback to being the coach. You're still a vital part of each game (each day at the shop), but you're not on the front lines anymore; you're just working closely with the people who are. If you grow to multiple shops, you become the owner of the team. You hire all the right people, make your vision and goals clear, and then stay out of their way, trusting them to get the job done and to ask for help when they need it. This is your new role.

2. Make Sure You Have the Cash

The next and often biggest challenge of growth is cash flow. If you're going to grow, you need to have a lot of money or you need to have access to a lot of money. It's interesting to hear people talk about a new shop. They seem to talk only about how much money they can *make*. What they seem to forget is how much money they can *lose*. Simply put, if you're set up to make money by the wheelbarrowful, you're set up to lose that same amount of money. It's critical that you have backup plans in place to get money from somewhere if you should happen to lose that wheelbarrowful of money.

And this is exactly why a good relationship with a banker is so important. Odds are pretty good that you won't have the necessary money sitting in an account somewhere. Financing for properties and lines of credit for equipment and emergencies are vital. Never underestimate how much money it will take to open a new shop.

Still with me? Still up for the challenge of opening a new shop? OK, then let's look at how to do it.

3. Pick a Location and Negotiate Your Best Deal

First, pick a location. The best locations are within a ten- to twenty-minute drive of your existing shop. That's because you'll need to be able to travel quickly and easily between the two locations—especially if this is your first attempt at expansion. This will make the adjustment to your new role a lot easier. It also will allow you to get back in and get your hands dirty if the need arises.

Once you've picked your location, you'll want to negotiate for the space. My favorite way to do this is with a lease option agreement. You want to lease the property, but you want an agreed-upon time frame and purchase price at which you can buy the property at a later date. At the beginning it's also good to ask for several months' rent free. Many property owners will be happy to oblige if they think you'll be a long-term tenant and ultimately may buy the property.

When negotiating a lease or a purchase, the best way to come up with a fair price is to figure out what the property is worth to you. How much money do you expect to make with a shop on that property? To put it simply, what's the most you can pay for the property and still make money? With this number in mind you'll be armed for negotiations with a clear idea of what will work for you.

A well-run shop can make a lot of money. So it is possible to pay top dollar *if you have to* and still be satisfied with your investment.

It's also a good idea to put a "bailout clause" in your lease. A bailout clause says that for a certain dollar amount (usually between $5,000-$10,000) you can walk away from the lease and options. The seller/lesser probably will be happy to add this clause because it assures him that you're not going to just disappear on him if things don't work out. And it's good for you because if things really don't work out, you are not trapped in a long-term lease that you can't afford.

4. Find the Best People

This brings us to the next challenge of growth: people. To grow effectively, you've got to have the best people, not just the right people. The quality of your employees has to go up a notch when you open a second location. Instead of just being on time and friendly, these employees have to be smart, loyal, honest, able to make decisions, and incredibly reliable. Without employees like this, a second shop will be very difficult, if not impossible, to manage. Such employees take time and effort to find and to train. And then you have to pay more to get them and to keep them. This means that while you're negotiating for the lease, you also will be interviewing for employees. Believe me, you never can start this process too early.

Remember, you now need high-caliber employees for both locations. Give yourself as much time as possible to find them. One option is to bring one or two key employees from your first shop over to the new shop. This can work, but be careful. The money you are making in your first shop is the money that is giving you the power to expand. If you're going to pull one or two key employees out of that shop, make darn sure you're not hurting the shop's profitability. Nothing is worse than having your main shop start to struggle just as you are trying to open the second one.

When bringing people into a second location, it's also a good idea to develop in them an ownership mentality. There are two ways to do this. You either can make one of them a part-owner or you can show them all how they can become part-owners if they perform at certain levels. The right person will jump at an opportunity for ownership, especially if you have a track record of success.

If you find someone like this, make it easy for him. Shop owners have a tendency to make it difficult by asking for a huge financial investment (which the employee is unlikely to be able to afford) or a ridiculous buy-in period (very few people are going to wait for a five-year buy-in these days). If you have someone you consider ownership material, make it as easy and inexpensive as possible for him to become a partner. If you really do have the right person, you'll be richly rewarded with additional profits, not to mention the peace of mind that comes with knowing that your interests and his interests are the same.

5. Open for Business

Once you've picked your location, negotiated the lease options, and found your employees, it's time to move in and open for business.

People often spend ridiculous amounts of money getting ready to work instead of working. Here's the rule: Spend as little money as possible to get the doors open, and get the doors open as soon as possible.

All you really need is a floor jack and a case of oil from Wal-Mart! (I'm kidding, but not by much.) Spend enough to get a great sign. This will be the face of your business for years. Put a good paint job on the building and make sure the landscaping is in tip-top shape. Remember, this is long-term advertising.

Make sure the intake/waiting area is clean but not fancy (you want to discourage waiting, not encourage it). When it comes to equipment, start with the minimum number of lifts you need to get up and running. Purchase tire machines, alignment machines, etc., as needed. Try to convince manufacturers and suppliers to provide any special equipment that might be necessary to use their services. Even if your cash situation is good, try to get leases or financing on your equipment. Always negotiate for no prepayment penalties so that you conserve your cash for the start-up period (but can pay off the equipment anytime you want to). The whole key is to get started as inexpensively as possible; spending $10,000–$20,000 is a good target range.

Make sure all your best customer service systems are in place from the very beginning. Your new customers' experiences will be the most powerful marketing tool you have when you open a second shop. A few good words from some extremely satisfied customers, and you're off and running. A few bad experiences at the beginning, and you create a huge obstacle you'll have to overcome.

6. Don't Waste Time and Money on a "Grand Opening" Day

Get the doors open as soon as possible. This means as soon as you have a technician and a lift. Delaying the opening just increases your risk and decreases your odds of success.

Too many times people put a lot of time and effort into a "grand opening." Grand openings aren't a bad marketing tool, but don't bet the farm on them. Grand openings in independent auto repair shops usually don't generate a lot of immediate income (you can easily generate more business than you can handle). If you really want to have a grand-opening celebration, try a grand-opening month, with fantastic specials all month long. This will be a lot more effective than spending a whole bunch of marketing money on just a one- or two-day event.

Once you're open for business, it's just like operating your existing shop. Transfer and implement the same great systems that have created profitability at your main location. Repeat this process until you have as many shops as you'd like to have.

CHAPTER 11

Exit Strategies

So you've built an empire. Now how do you get out? What's your exit strategy, whether you have one shop or many?

Why Do You Want to Get Out?

You knew I was going to ask this. Unless you're dealing with illness, divorce, or some other major life disruption, you may prefer to step back from the business without exactly exiting. If you're burned out, try taking some time off. If you've lost your passion, try focusing on developing your people. Sometimes the process of giving something back through mentoring can recharge your batteries and get you fired up again.

Options for Getting Out without Selling

OK, so you're sure you want to get out of the daily operations of your business. How do you do it? Before you consider an outright sale, give these other options a look:

1. Partnership

2. License

3. Franchise

Disclaimer: Each of these options is subject to federal, state, and local laws and regulations. The discussion here is not intended as legal or financial advice. Before taking any of these steps, or any other steps, you need to check with your attorney and accountant. The risk is yours, so do your due diligence.

1. Partnership

Partnership is one way to exit your business. The right partner can give you your freedom while allowing you stay involved and possibly even retain control of your business. The right partner also will have skills that complement yours. When you form a partnership, be sure you make it clear that you want to step back and be less involved. This will be a fantastic opportunity for your new partner. I have been on both sides of this type of transaction. I've been the person who comes in and sets someone free from a business, and I've been the one seeking partners so that I could be free. With the right people involved, this arrangement can be ideal.

The important thing in a partnership is to clearly spell out the responsibilities and duties of the partners right from the start. And you'll need to spell out exactly what will happen if one partner wants to leave—or stops fulfilling his responsibilities. Lack of clarity in these areas can be very expensive, if not fatal, to the business.

2. Licensing

Licensing is quickly becoming an optimal way to grow or exit a business. Licensing has many of the benefits of franchising but without all the regulation and red tape. When you license your business, you give someone else permission to use the name and/or systems you've created. That person pays you a fee for this privilege. Of course, it's a privilege only if your business is successful! You then receive money from the business without being involved in the daily operations, while the licensee takes on most of the risk.

There are two disadvantages to licensing arrangements. One is that you have less control over the final product than you would in a pure franchising agreement. The other disadvantage is that your brand must be perceived as valuable or you won't find anyone willing to be your licensee.

3. Franchising

Franchising is a very popular and proven way to grow and/or exit your business once you've developed an effective brand and system. This is the exit strategy that I prefer. The big advantage is that there's less risk for your main business. Most of the risk is transferred to the franchisees. Also, you can operate a very large business with a very small staff. I was able to operate twenty-one stores with a staff of four people. Finally, with a franchise, you maintain a lot of control over the final product.

The disadvantages are cost and franchisee management. Franchising is highly regulated, which means that there are substantial legal fees involved in setting up a franchise. Once you've taken care of the setup, there's the issue of franchisees. There's a saying in the franchise business: "At the beginning they need you and love you; after five years they think they did it all by themselves." You constantly will be recruiting, training, supporting, and replacing franchisees. How well you do these things and whether you enjoy doing them determine your success as a franchisor.

Outright Sale

Maybe none of the options above is for you. After thinking it over, you decide you want to do an outright sale. How do you do this?

When you sell your business, you'll have two possible buyers: an outsider and an insider.

To sell to an outsider, you list the business for sale with a broker and/or on the Internet, and then you start showing it to prospective buyers. The advantage of selling to an outsider is that there is no relationship. It purely is a business deal. Outsiders will buy or not buy based on what they believe to be the value of the business. If your ad is not misleading, an outsider can be a good match for the business in terms of risk tolerance, experience, and financial situation. This matters because someone who likes the deal will complete it quickly and with little or no financing or other complications, such as a long-term consulting arrangement.

There are also disadvantages to working with an outside buyer. An outsider may not appreciate the value of your business. He may not trust your numbers or he simply may not understand your business well enough to accurately evaluate it. In either of these cases, it will be hard to complete a sale with this person. Another disadvantage is with information sharing. During the sale process you may be asked for information about your business that you consider to be trade secrets. Putting this information into the hands of an outsider, even with all kinds of legal disclaimers, can be unnerving and even damaging.

The other option, of course, is selling to an insider. This is the option I've used and seen used most often and most effectively. An insider already knows everything he needs to know about the business to make a purchase decision. An insider intimately understands the risks and opportunities. An insider understands the true value of the business, including the hard-to-quantify intangibles. And since he already has relationships with your key employees and suppliers, an insider is more likely to operate the business successfully.

There are, however, a few disadvantages to selling to an insider. An insider often doesn't have the cash or credit available to complete the transaction, so you end up having to finance the deal. And he may need extensive coaching and consulting from you before he can make the transition from employee to owner. Finally, the existing relationship can cloud judgment on both sides, leading to a deal that is unfair to one party or the other, even if unintentionally so.

Structuring a Sale

Whether you decide to sell to an outsider or to an insider, the structure of the deal is very important. Needless to say, the more money you can get up front, the better. An all-cash deal at closing is the best scenario. If the buyer doesn't have the cash, make sure you approach several banks to fund the sale. And don't forget about the Small Business Administration (SBA). The SBA can be a great source of funds for someone attempting to become a new business owner.

A final option is for you to "hold a note," or finance part of the deal. This can be risky, so make sure that everyone is clear about the collateral—usually it's the business as well as assets. Ideally, the buyer personally will guarantee any notes to you. If he is not willing to do this, you seriously should consider not going through with the deal.

Another critical thing to make clear is the consequence to the buyer if he stops paying you. If the business is your collateral and the buyer stops paying, time is of the essence when it comes to getting the business back into your hands. So be sure your agreement allows you to move quickly. I've seen shop owners watch their collateral get destroyed by someone who wasn't paying them, and there was nothing they could do because their agreements were poorly written. Make sure the agreement has some teeth in it. Don't be shy about spending money on quality lawyers at this point. Penalties for not performing as agreed should be as severe as the law allows. Everyone needs to be motivated to honor the agreement.

Once an agreement has been reached, close the deal as quickly as possible. Delaying the closing only increases the odds of complications or surprises that could derail the deal from being completed.

CHAPTER 12

Vision and Goals

I'll always remember that very first day at my new shop. As I turned the key in the lock and opened the door, I had a vision (OK, so it was more of a daydream than a vision) of being wealthy and retired in six months. Little did I know what was really in store for me. There was so much I didn't know back then. Instead of pausing to clarify my vision, my goals, and my strategy, I dove right into problem solving.

I inherited all the service writers and technicians with my shop, and they were full of advice for their new boss. "We need all kinds of new equipment." I bought it. "We work too many hours." I shortened the work day. "We're not making enough money." I gave them all guarantees. "The customers are all cheapskates." I lowered the prices on everything. "We need to use dealer parts on all jobs." I did.

Needless to say, the money started going out faster than it was coming in. A lot faster. All because I started by focusing on problem solving (and taking advice from the wrong people) before I figured out my vision and goals.

Almost anyone you talk to will tell you that you need to have goals. Those same people also will tell you that having a vision is a good idea. And when they tell you this, you probably just nod your head in agreement. Everybody agrees that vision and goals are important. But how many people are sure what a vision or goal looks like? The good news is that both concepts are easy to understand and simple to implement. It's like repairing a car. If you follow a logical series of steps, you should get the desired result. Setting my vision and goals was the first step in slingshotting myself from desperate and broke to successful and wealthy. By setting your vision and goals, you'll move closer to the success and wealth you deserve.

So let's get started. What's your vision? What goals have you set to realize that vision?

Default Mode Vision

Your answers to the following questions are the first, most important steps in the creation of a fantastically profitable auto repair shop. Once you have these questions answered, the actions required will be obvious. Most shop owners have never even thought about these questions, let alone answered them. Let's take them one at a time.

What's your vision? At this point many people ask, "Personal or professional?" Good question. The answer is simple, and yes, it's the obvious one: personal. I've worked with too many shop owners who were owned by their businesses instead of the other way around. The small, happy little shops they started out with had turned into huge, evil, life-swallowing monsters that they no longer could control. All because they never thought about their personal visions. People who don't figure out their personal visions go into "default vision mode." What's the default? It's simple, seductive, and dangerous: faster, bigger, more! That's the "vision" most people use to guide their lives. Heck, that's what I used in the beginning, before experience taught me a few hard lessons. The very simplicity of this vision is what makes it the default. You don't have to think too much. You don't have to plan. Best of all, you get lots of positive feedback from the people around you if you operate in faster, bigger, more mode. Even if you're not really happy while doing it!

Four Vision-Defining Questions

You deserve to be happy *and* profitable. That's why you're reading this book. So, how do you identify your personal vision? The best way is to ask yourself four important questions.

1. If you won the lottery, would you keep doing what you're doing?

2. Are you excited about getting into the office each morning?

3. What do you like most about what you do?

4. What do you like least about what you do?

If your answer to the first two questions is "No!" you'll most likely be doing something else within five years, unless you have a superhuman tolerance for misery. Trust me on that. So you have a choice to make. Do you let things unfold in the faster, bigger, more default mode, or do you take charge and make some conscious changes? It's up to you.

If you answered yes to the first two questions, you're probably in the right place, doing the right thing. In that case, let's move on to the next two questions. The key to setting a useful vision is figuring out what you enjoy and what you don't enjoy, and then structuring your life so that you get more of what you like and less of what you don't. Once you get the hang of it, the process really is quite simple.

I don't like tomatoes. I never order them and I want them left out of anything I do order. I organize my life so that I rarely run into a tomato, except in an unrecognizable form (ketchup, spaghetti sauce, etc.).

One thing I do love is sushi. I'll go for weeks eating nothing but sushi. I seek it out. I invent reasons to eat it. I do everything I can to make it a regular part of my life.

I hate details, paperwork, and lawyers, (with very few exceptions sorry, guys). I structure my life to avoid these bothersome things at all costs. I have a bookkeeper and an accountant to handle details. I personally deal with very little paperwork. As for lawyers, I try to avoid all situations that require their presence. If I have to deal with them, I do it with a very tight agenda and I hold the meetings standing up (they get tired and end the meetings that much sooner).

With the exception of lawyers, I love people. I love communicating with my clients by email, on the phone, or in person. I enjoy it because I can produce results. I can use my experience and training to help them make phenomenal changes in their lives and their businesses, and that gives me a huge rush. So I structured my life in such a way that I'm working with my clients 90 percent of the time.

I do all these things—run from tomatoes, eat sushi every day, meet lawyers in chairless rooms, and spend as much time as possible with my clients—because I've answered the important questions and I know what works for me. Vision setting is all about making clear to yourself what you really want in your life, now and in the future. Once you're clear, you can turn your vision into goals that will create action now.

For instance, in the example above I admitted how much I like sushi. I even stated a sushi vision: seeking it out and making it a regular part of my life. The next step would be to set a goal for sushi. It would look like this: "It's 6 p.m. on August 3 and I am eating sushi at Kiku Sushi Restaurant at 6 p.m. As always, I'm happily enjoying the pleasure it gives me and how fulfilled I feel as I eat it."

A common vision statement is: "My vision is to make a lot of money!" That begs the next question: "Why do you want to make a lot of money?" Usually, I get either a blank stare or something along the lines of, "Um ... so I can buy stuff?" Let's talk about making money.

More and Why: Is Your Vision to Make Money?

We open businesses in the hope and belief that we will be able to offer something of value to the world and thereby make money. But why is making money so important to us? Because that's the way we were raised. Our parents and grandparents suffered through the Great Depression. Most of them were touched by it in some way, and the message they got was, "You never can have enough money." They did a good job of passing this imperative on to us. This is the origin of the "more" in the default vision mode of faster, bigger, more.

The other part of "more" comes from marketers and society as a whole. We are bombarded every day with messages that tell us we'll be happy if we drive a certain car, live in a certain house, use a certain brand of deodorant. We may resist those messages, but then we visit friends who tell us about their fantastic cars, houses, deodorants ... and we feel the need to keep up. It's a vicious cycle.

Let me be clear: I have nothing against "stuff" (I love all my really cool expensive electronic gadgets). The important thing is to have a vision and goals for your life and then to make sure those are supported by your buying habits.

Most people are so focused on "more" that they don't stop to figure out "why," much less "enough." I was one of those people for much of my life. But once you figure out "why" and "enough," your personal vision will start to come into focus.

One last thought about "more" and "why." There was a great study done by two Princeton professors, economist Alan B. Krueger and psychologist and Nobel laureate Daniel

Kahneman, in 2006. The study found that up to an income of about $50,000 a year, there is a direct link between income and happiness. Above that number, more money does not make people happier! The authors concluded that because of the illusion that money can buy happiness, people waste time doing things like spending too many hours commuting to work (the least happy activity, according to the study) that they otherwise could invest in socializing with people they like (the most happiness-producing activity).

Pay attention to this finding; it's important. Simply figuring out what "enough" is for you (beyond just money) can be the foundation upon which you build a very satisfying life and business.

Getting through the Problems and to the Vision

People who come to me generally have a problem to be solved. To them it's a very big problem. They are scared, they are beat up financially and emotionally, and they do not know what to do. The good news is that there are very few problems that can't be solved. (Remember, I had twenty-one shops; there aren't many problems that I haven't seen). So the first order of business is for me to help these people solve this tremendous problem that drove them to seek my advice in the first place. Once we get the big problem solved (this usually takes less than three months), we immediately start talking about their visions and goals, because the way to prevent big problems is to have visions and goals.

If you lack a clear vision, every problem is a big problem. With vision comes perspective. With proper perspective, problems are appropriately sized and suddenly become manageable. So, here are some tools.

Setting Goals to Support Your Vision:
A Powerful Tool

Many years ago, I was trying to do some personal goal setting. In the past, I always had written things down on index cards. This worked great. But the Internet was coming to life and I figured, why not put it to work for this powerful purpose? From this humble beginning came the website www.mygoalguide.com. It's designed specifically to do two things: help you write down your goals in a simple, organized fashion, and remind you of your goals on a daily basis by emailing them to you up to three times a day.

The site uses the concept of major life categories. There is an important reason for this. Back in the 1980s, when I first was introduced to goal setting, I put the process to use immediately. The results were fantastic. Unfortunately, the only area of my life I used it for was my income. Sure enough, my income doubled every year for several years, but I wasn't happy. I figured that if I could just use this goal-setting thing to get a little more money, I'd be happy. It never happened. I never really started to feel happy and satisfied until I learned to set goals in *all* areas of my life. To help you avoid the mistake I made, I've provided categories for all areas of your life.

When I first created this site, nothing like it existed. Now hundreds of people use it every day. I've never used advertising on the site or sent spam to anyone who has signed up. The site is totally free—money-free and hassle-free—for you to use. Try it now.

For those of you who prefer to write goals the old-fashioned way, here is the short course. To be effective, goals need to have five key characteristics.

Five Goal-Setting Characteristics

1. Goals must be specific. the more specific the better. Not "I want to be rich." Instead, "I want to have $1 million in the bank."

2. Goals must be believable to you. Can you see yourself in the picture?

3. Goals must have due dates. For example, "By December 20XX, I will have $1 million in my Bank of America money market account."

4. Goals must be measurable. Earning $1 million certainly meets this requirement.

5. Goals must be stated in the first-person present tense. "I have" instead of "I will have."

Let's talk a little more about each of these characteristics.

1. Goals Must Be Specific

A goal that isn't specific isn't a goal. It's a wish. Goal setting works because you are painting a picture for yourself. If I say, "Let's go get a hamburger," you might say, "Sure, whatever." If I say instead, "Let's go get two all-beef patties, special sauce, lettuce, cheese, pickles, onions on a sesame seed bun," you'd say, "Let's go!" Why? Because I painted a complete, delicious picture for you. It's not just a hamburger, it's something special you can almost taste just from the description. The same thing is true when you set a goal. The more specific, the more vivid, the more accurately you can describe your goal, the more likely you are to achieve it. Another example: "I want to win a car." Compare that to: "I am driving the fast and sexy bright-red 1968 Chevy Camaro that I won from Dave Dickson in the 2006 Shop Owner's Best of the Best contest." See how different it feels?

2. Goals Must Be Believable to You

You'll sometimes hear people say, "You've got to set a BHAG" (which stands for big hairy audacious goal). They say you should set goals that really stretch you and push you. This is true but only to a point. There are a few BHAGs on my goal list, but there are a whole lot more less-audacious goals: ones that I can see, feel, and taste. Your BHAGs should be out there on the edge, perhaps just a notch below winning the lottery. If you achieve them, the world is yours. But it's the smaller, more believable goals that will drive your daily actions and make your life rich. Make sure that most of the goals on your list are believable to you. You don't have to know exactly how you're going to achieve them, but you must be able to see yourself in the picture.

3. Goals Must Have Due Dates

Why is this so important? Because most of us are born to procrastinate. Don't feel bad if you have this problem; it's normal. Without some internal or external pressure, we're likely to put things off as long as possible, even things that are good for us. Due dates solve this problem. A due date forces action. It creates urgency and responsibility. It will make your "inner overachiever" kick in. Try it; you'll be pleasantly surprised. This is a great place to throw in a "black belt" goal-setting skill. If you really want to increase the odds of hitting your goal, add some serious rocket fuel. Share your goal and your due date with somebody who cares about you. The pressure to perform, to succeed in someone else's eyes, will do wonders. You'll find unbelievably creative solutions to problems that normally would stop you cold. This is a great bonus strategy.

4. Goals Must Be Measurable

You've gotta know exactly what you're shooting for. Not approximately. Not sorta kinda. *Exactly.* The more precise and measurable your goals, the more likely you are to achieve them. Instead of "I will have $1 million in the bank," try "I will have exactly $1,238,658 in the bank." It may sound like I'm splitting hairs here; I'm not. There is a method to my madness. You see, the more precise and measurable the goal, the more believable it is. The more believable it is, the more likely you are to achieve it. You've got to believe, and exact, measurable goals make this easier.

5. Goals Must Be Stated in the First-Person Present Tense

This one is a lot like the measurable rule. The whole reason for this is to make your goal real. This changes it from a wish ("I want to") to a reality ("I will"). This may seem like a simple word game, but believe me, it's not. It's much more than that. This is the magic. "Owning" the words by saying them as if they already have happened magnifies their power one hundred times. Always state your goals in the first-person present tense. Simply put, say them as if they already are a reality.

Turbo Charging Your Goal-Setting Results

There are some secrets you can use to dramatically increase the chances of achieving your goals.
- Write your goals down on paper.
- Tell others what your goals are.
- Get other people involved in helping you achieve your goals.

- Help other people achieve *their* goals.

Writing things down actually helps burn them into your brain. It's good to use electronic tools as well, but nothing will set your goals in your memory like writing them down on paper.

Telling others your goals makes you accountable. It's easy to sleep in and not work out if you're going to the gym by yourself. But set an appointment to meet someone there, and all of a sudden you are accountable and much more likely to show up. This is a powerful tool.

Other people's involvement magnifies the power of your goals. Most people are afraid to ask for help. That's a shame, because if you ask, you'll be amazed at how helpful most people will be. Getting others involved makes your goals much bigger and more powerful. The people helping you have an investment in your success. You are no longer alone.

Finally, helping others achieve their goals invokes the principle of reciprocity. When you help them, they will help you. The key is not to help someone because you're *expecting* them to help you. Just help them with no expectations and see what happens. This is the most powerful of all the tools for achieving your goals.

The five goal-setting characteristics and four secrets I set forth in this chapter are all you need to remember to effectively set and achieve goals in all areas of your life. The best way to create the success you want and achieve the goals you've set is to accomplish something relating to each of your goals every day. To do this, you'll be utilizing all the resources (tools, people, and systems) that we've covered.

By coupling all the resources addressed in this book with a clear vision and goals, you can create the slingshot experience you deserve in your business.

BONUS CHAPTER

The Power of Mastermind

You now have in your hands the tools you need to create your own slingshot experience. You can go to www.DavidDickson.com/guide to get any of the resources I've mentioned in this book. However, nobody achieves success on his or her own. We all need a little help.

Let's talk about my secret weapon. In 1908, Napoleon Hill was a reporter assigned to interview Andrew Carnegie (the richest man in the world at the time) for a series of articles about famous men. During the interview, Hill uncovered Carnegie's philosophy that the process of success could be spelled out in a simple formula and could be duplicated by the average person. Carnegie was impressed with Hill and commissioned him (without pay and only offering to provide him with letters of reference) to interview more than 500 successful men and women, many of them millionaires, in order to flesh out and then publish this formula for success.

As part of his research, Hill interviewed many of the most famous people of the time, including Thomas Edison, Alexander Graham Bell, George Eastman, Henry Ford, John D. Rockefeller, Charles M. Schwab, F.W. Woolworth, William Wrigley, Jr., William Jennings Bryan, Joseph Stalin,

Theodore Roosevelt, William H. Taft, Woodrow Wilson, and many, many more. The project lasted more than twenty years. The ultimate result of Hill's project was the groundbreaking book "Think and Grow Rich." In this book, Hill identified fifteen Laws of Success. These are the things that super-successful individuals do to create their success. We're not going to look at all fifteen here. However, in working with auto repair shop owners all over the country, I have discovered that super-successful shop owners all share five characteristics identified by Hill.

The Five Key Characteristics of Successful People Are:

1. Burning Desire

2. Specialized Knowledge

3. Decisive Nature

4. Goal-Oriented Mind-Set

5. Mastermind Group

1. Burning Desire

If you want to be successful in the auto repair business, you must have a burning desire to be successful. You must be passionate about helping people. To be truly successful, you must get up every morning excited and energized by the prospect of facing and overcoming the challenges of running your shop. Every year, I talk two or three people out of buying an auto repair shop because they don't have this burning desire. If the desire isn't there, the results will be disappointing. The good news is that if you are reading this book and you've come this far, you almost certainly have the burning desire to succeed!

2. Specialized Knowledge

The second key characteristic is that you must have specialized knowledge. You must know something that others don't and be able to act on what you know. This book is filled with specialized knowledge. If you've read this far, stop and congratulate yourself. You have acquired specialized knowledge that less than 1 percent of the shop owners in America possess. The only thing you have to do now is put the knowledge you have acquired into action!

3. Decisive Nature

Next, you must be decisive. You cannot be successful without the ability to make decisions. The good news is that the decisions don't always have to be correct. Super-successful shop owners understand that any decision is better than no decision at all. They understand that they always can recover from mistakes, but they can't always recreate lost opportunities. We are trained to "think about it," "sleep on it," "give it time." But super-successful shop owners know that this advice is bad advice. When someone who is this successful is presented with an opportunity, even one surrounded by uncertainty, he simply says, "I'll take it!" He trusts himself and the people around him to figure out the details later.

4. Goal-Oriented Mind-Set

Super-successful auto repair shop owners know where they are going and have plans to get there. Without goals, the work is meaningless. Without goals, the burning desire fades. Goals are the key to creating success for yourself and your team. As we saw in the last chapter, the process of setting goals may be simple, but it's incredibly powerful. To be truly successful, you must have goals. (Use the website I created to help you: www.mygoalguide.com.)

5. Mastermind Group

This is the most important step in the process of becoming a super-successful auto repair shop owner. My success skyrocketed when I fully understood and applied this principle. You can't do it alone. There is too much information. Business today literally evolves at the speed of light (the Internet). There is no way you can keep track of everything. You must have the best possible mastermind group that you can assemble around you at all times. This group will give you knowledge, wisdom, perspective, and motivation.

There should be several types of people in your personal mastermind group. We're not going to discuss them all here, but the most important type of person is the wise and experienced one who already has had success in your industry. In other words, super-successful auto repair shop owners surround themselves with other super-successful auto repair shop owners. With enough wise and experienced owners on your team, you won't come across any business problems that somebody hasn't seen and handled successfully in the past.

Creating these kinds of mastermind teams is something I have been doing for years. Most shop owners don't get out much, so they don't have time to identify and connect with other super-successful shop owners. So I do it for them. I carefully screen people and put them together in powerful mastermind groups. The results are phenomenal. Slingshot events occur regularly. If you are decisive and want to be part of one of these powerful, super-successful groups of shop owners, go to www.DavidDickson.com/mastermind. If you qualify and are accepted, the benefits will be life changing. You will have access to the knowledge, wisdom, perspective, and motivation to achieve any goal you set. This final tool has been my "secret weapon." Now it can be yours.

LaVergne, TN USA
27 December 2010
210150LV00002B/1/P